Devotion to the Mother of God

by

W. Doyle Gilligan

Lumen Christi Press
Houston, Texas 77219

Printed in the United States of America
for Lumen Christi Press
P.O. Box 130176
Houston, Texas 77219

Nihil Obstat:
Reverend Monsignor James L. Golasinski

Imprimatur:
Most Reverend Joseph A. Fiorenza
Bishop of Galveston-Houston
June 4, 1997

First Printing: June 1997

Copyright 1997 by W. Doyle Gilligan

Library of Congress
Catalog Card Number: 97-072619
Lumen Christi: ISBN 0-912-414-61-8

Cover: The painting of the Annunciation hangs over a side altar in the Basilica of the Annunciation in Nazareth. It is very close to the spot where the Archangel Gabriel announced to Mary that she would become the Mother of God.

Contents

Introduction
1. Mary, Mother of God and Our Mother 1
2. Marian Prayers 28
3. Prayers of the Saints and Holy People to the Blessed Virgin 41
4. Feasts of Our Lady 54
5. Our Lady in the Bible 62
6. Apparitions of Our Lady 82
7. Marian Hymns 103
8. Special Devotions 114
9. Aspirations 120
10. Mary Leads Us to the Eucharist — Pope John Paul II 122
11. Our Lady and Vatican II 127
    Bibliography 149

Dedication

*To Mary, Mother of God, who looks after all of us;
to my sisters, Mary Sheahan and Helen Torpy;
to Elizabeth and Paul O'Connell;
with whom I returned to Nazareth.*

All generations will call me blessed: The Church's devotion to the Blessed Virgin is intrinsic to Christian worship. The Church rightly honors the Blessed Virgin with a special devotion. From the most ancient times the Blessed Virgin has been honored with the title of Mother of God, to whose protection the faithful fly in all their dangers and needs . . .

Catechism of the Catholic Church #197

Introduction

This book—*Devotion to Mary, Mother of God*—is just an introduction to the Blessed Virgin. I hope that it will encourage the reader to dig deeper by reading, at least some of the books I have listed in the bibliography. So many great books have been written on Mary and so many more will continue to be written as long as time exists.

There never was a saint who did not have a great devotion to Mary. One might say, the greater devotion, the greater the saint. St Louis de Montfort said that no one could reach intimate union with Jesus unless he had the closest bonds with Mary. Pope Paul VI said: *Our Lady is the road that leads us safely to Christ.* Another time he said that Christ has come to us through Mary and we have received him from her. If we want to be true Christians we must recognize the vital relationship which exists between Jesus and Mary, and see how this union of Son and Mother is the way which leads us to him.

No matter how far we are away from Christ and his Church, Mary can bring us back. It is her mission. She wants everyone to reach salvation and is willing to give more than a helping hand if we ask. Again St Louis de Montfort says that Mary is the mediatrix and intercessor between men and her Son, while Jesus is our mediator with the Father. (*True Devotion #80*)

In the chapter *Our Lady and Vatican II*, I show how devotion to Mary has been very much emphasized by the council. And I end the first chapter pointing out how the saints and the great spiritual writers of the Church from the very beginning have held that Mary is the channel of all graces.

If this book will help just a little to get the reader to deepen his or her devotion, and perhaps encourage others to do the same, I will be happy. For that reason, I have listed some of the devotions to Our Lady, and some of the reasons that Christ's Church encourages us to use these devotions. There are certain days when the Church celebrates the glories of Mary. Some feasts are greater than others, but the encouragement is always there. Every Saturday is set aside to give special honor to Mary, and the first Saturday of each month is a special day to honor her under the title which her Son loves—the Sorrowful and Immaculate Heart of Mary.

We can learn so much from Our Blessed Mother. She who wants to be a mother to each of us, is also a model for us to imitate. We can look at her virtues one by one and see how she acts. We, little by little, can follow her example. We see that her first virtue is that of obedience, when she, at the Annunciation, accepts God's will unconditionally.

Our Lady revealed to St Bridget that through the merit of her obedience she had obtained so great power that no sinner, however great his crimes, who had recourse to her with a desire to amend his ways, failed to obtain pardon.

We can see all the other virtues manifested in the Gospel passages which portray her life. Starting with obedience to the will of God, we can add virtue by virtue until we become true children of Mary and like her realize a happiness and peace which comes only by being active followers of Christ.

Mary certainly wants each of us to be happy now and hereafter in heaven. She more than any human, other than her Son, knows the true meaning of life—to know, love and serve God in this world, and to be happy with him forever in the next. Our lives will have meaning when we realize this and begin to put it into practice. Mary, our Mother, can be our help. We will be able to endure the suffering that life brings, the contradictions, the failures, the crosses; and yet we will be able to put them into their true perspective and be happy. Again Our Lady shows us by her life! She had her sorrows but she accepted them as the will of God and she was happy. She is the most successful woman that ever lived. She had the greatest task of any woman and accomplished it with perfection. St Louis de Montfort tells us that Mary has given more glory to God than all the angels and saints have given him or ever will give him. We, in our ordinary lives can imitate Mary and turn all our actions into prayer.

W. Doyle Gilligan
March 25, 1997

1

Mary, Mother of God and Our Mother

The most awesome place in the whole world is in the center of Nazareth a town in Galalee. Although Nazareth is located in the middle of the land of the Bible, it is not mentioned in the Old Testament. Now, for two thousand years it shines forth like the brightest of stars - the sun - beaconing all to come and see where God the Son was conceived - where the greatest event in history took place.

A young woman called Mary was visited by the Archangel Gabriel. He came from God to tell her that she was to become the Mother of the Savior, the second person of the Blessed Trinity, by the power of the Holy Spirit. She gave her *fiat*, her yes, to the will of God and by her obedience, as the handmaid of the Lord she conceived. *The Word was made flesh* and the great moment, which would be captured thousands of times by all the great artists from the beginning of Christian art - the Incarnation, took place. There is not an art museum in the western world that does not display, at least one picture of the Annunciation.

And if one walks around the best art museums in the world one will find that Mary is very much there. One can hear echos of the *Magnificat*, the psalm recited by Mary when she meets her cousin St Elizabeth - *All generations shall call me blessed.*

This young Jewish woman wanted to live a life known to God - to spend her earthly years giving glory to her creator in simple prayer. That was her plan. It was not God's plan.

I knelt in the place where Mary was told God's plan by the angel. I was alone. I bent and kissed the spot below the phrase, *Verbum caro hic factum est* (here the Word was made flesh) displayed at the foot of a small altar. It was not difficult for me to realize that I was in the most famous spot in the created universe - I felt a great nearness to Jesus and his Mother. But I know that we are even closer to Jesus and Mary when any day, anywhere in the world we receive the Blessed Eucharist - the Body, Blood, Soul and Divinity of Our Lord the Son of Mary.

The Antiphon for the Mass of the Blessed Virgin for Saturday is *Hail, holy Mother! The child to whom you gave birth is the King of heaven and earth forever.* It is enough for us to realize the power of Mary - the influence she has with her Son. G. K. Chesterton paints the majesty of Christ in a little poem.

> The Christ-child lay on Mary's lap,
> > His hair was like a light.
> (O weary, weary were the world,
> > But here is all aright.)

> The Christ-child lay on Mary's breast,
> > His hair was like a star.
> (O stern and cunning are the kings,
> > But here the true hearts are.)

> The Christ-child lay on Mary's heart,
> > His hair was like a fire.
> (O weary, weary is the world,
> > But here the world's desire.)

> The Christ-child stood on Mary's knee,
> > His hair was like a crown.

And all the flowers looked up at Him,
    And all the stars looked down.

The young Jewish woman who wanted to live a simple life, away forever from the glare of the world's notice, did live a simple life, but one which would be remembered forever as long as the world remains and for all eternity. When her earthly life ended she was taken up to heaven where she was crowned Queen of the Universe. However, she prefers that we call her Mother and she wants us to treat her as a mother.

In a general audience on January 3, 1996, the Holy Father, Pope John Paul II said: *Our lives are profoundly influenced by Mary's example and intercession. Nonetheless, we must ask ourselves about our efforts to be close to her. The entire teaching of salvation history invites us to look to the Virgin. Christian asceticism in every age invites us to think of her as a model of perfect adherence to the Lord's will. The chosen model of holiness, Mary guides the steps of believers on their journey to heaven.*

Through her closeness to the events of our daily history, Mary sustains us in trials; she encourages us in difficulty, always pointing out to us the goal of eternal salvation. Thus her role as Mother is seen even more clearly; Mother of her Son Jesus, tender and vigilant Mother to each one of us, to whom, from the cross, the Redeemer entrusted her, that we might welcome her as children in faith.

St Aelred, a Cistertian of the 12th century, writing about Our Lady, said that he who fails to honor the Mother clearly dishonors the Son. He went on to say, *She is our mother - mother of our life, the mother of our incarnation, the mother of our light . . . . She is more our mother than the mother of our flesh. Our birth from her is better, for from her is born our holiness, our wisdom, our justification, our redemption.*

It is not uncommon to see the great love a son has for his mother. If we see lack of love from a son, we consider it unnatural. Let us look at the son who has the greatest love for his mother; that great love pales in comparison with the love Jesus has for his Mother.

In the general audience on September 13, 1996, our Holy Father, Pope John Paul II said:

In the constitution Lumen gentium, the Council states that 'joined to Christ the head and in communion with all his saints, the faithful must in the first place, reverence the memory of the glorious ever Virgin Mary, Mother of God, and of our Lord Jesus Christ.' (#52) . . . .

In the disciples' eyes, as they gathered after the Ascension, the title Mother of Jesus acquires its full meaning. For them, Mary is a person unique in her kind: she received the singular grace of giving birth to the Savior of humanity; she lived for a long while at his side; and on Calvary she was called by the Crucified One to exercise a new motherhood in relation to the beloved disciple and, through him, to the whole Church.

The Council of Ephesus

It was at the Ecumenical Council of Ephesus, the third council of the Church, that the Blessed Virgin Mary was proclaimed the Mother of God. That was in 431. The ancient city of Ephesus stands in ruins on the coast of modern Turkey.

Jesus Christ, her Son, is both true God and true Man. This fact had always been held in the Church, but now it was stamped for all to believe. After the declaration of this dogma a basilica was dedicated in Rome in honor of Mary the Mother of God. It began to be called St Mary Major and is perhaps the oldest church in the west called after Our Lady.

All Catholics grow up being told that Our Blessed Lady, the Mother of the Second Person of the Holy Trinity, is our mother also. We are told the story from St John's Gospel where the dying Christ gave his Mother to his beloved apostle and gave his apostle to his Mother. And the apostle took her to his home. Tradition says that Our Lady lived for twelve years after the crucifixtion. And for many years she lived in a little house with St John, on a hill above the city of Ephesus. Now a little chapel stands where the house was supposed to have been.

I wonder how many Catholics understand what it is to love Mary as our mother. I suppose most realize it when a problem, particularly a human one, arises. It is always a good idea to turn to Mary and ask her help. Mary is ready to help us, her children. But do we know how she is our mother? We all know that we have a mother who nurtured us in her womb for nine months, gave birth to us and looked after us physically until we were able to do so ourselves. A mother in the natural order is the one person who has the greatest influence on one's life. Sometimes in our modern times that greatest gift a woman has is almost forgotten: that of being a full-time mother, giving her all to fulfill that most noble of vocations.

Our Lady is our mother in a very real sense - just as our natural mother is our greatest influence in the natural order, so is Mary our mother in the supernatural order. Our natural mother gives us life and is the first help with our physical well-being. Our Blessed Mother helps us with our supernatural life that was given to us by God in the sacrament of Baptism. Just as a good natural mother goes out of her way to see that her child is well looked after, and at an early age directed to the supernatural, so Our Lady, from the very beginning of one's existence, works for one's overall good - the priority being ultimate happiness with God the Father, God her Son and God the Holy Spirit in heaven for all eternity. *What does it profit a man if he gains the whole world, but loses his soul?*

Mary's consent was necessary in order that the Incarnation would take place. She answered a yes - her *fiat* - and *the Word was made flesh*, so that we could be redeemed by Christ, her Son, the God-man. When it came time for Christ to die for us, Mary was there at the foot of the cross, united to his sacrifice. Just as the Son offered himself to the Father for our salvation; Mary, too, joined in that offering. To make sure that we would know that Mary was our mother, Christ gave her to us as he was dying.

Our Lady was a powerful help to the apostles after the death of Christ. While it is not related in the gospels that Christ appeared to his Mother after he arose from the dead, surely it was to her, his great love, that he first appeared. Mary was with the apostles when the Holy Spirit, which she had already received, came upon them with the graces that Christ had promised. She was their mother and the Mother of the newly born Church. She continues to be the Mother of the Church. However, it was not until November 21, 1964, that Pope Paul VI, at the close of the third session of Vatican Council II, proclaimed *Mary the Mother of the Church, that is to say of all the people of God, of the faithful as well as the pastors, who call her the most loving Mother. And we wish that the Mother of God should be still more honored and involved by the entire Christian people of this most sweet title.*

The Immaculate Conception

As we get closer to eternity, God, through the Church makes things more clear to us. When the

Council of Ephesus declared that Mary was the Mother of God, it was the faithful who rejoiced in an exuberant way. They had always believed that Mary was the Mother of God. It was the theologians who argued among themselves, some saying no and others yes. God, through the Church, said yes! The riches of the Church is unfathomable because it is the Body of Christ and not just a great man-made organization to lead people to happiness and heaven. The more one gets to know the Church, the more beauty one sees; the more glorious it is; the more desire one has to become a better member of that Body which is Christ's.

The dogma of the Immaculate Conception was declared on December 8, 1854, by Pope Pius IX. After quoting many of the Fathers and Doctors of the Church as teaching this doctrine, St Alphonsus Liguori says: *Actually this opinion is defended by the universities of the Sorbonne, Salamanca, Coimbra, Cologne, Mainz, Naples and many others. All who take their degrees there are obliged to swear that they will defend the doctrine of Mary's Immaculate Conception. (The Glories of Mary*, Vol. 2, p. 16)

St Alphonsus tells a wonderful story in *The Glories of Mary*: There was a man who had not been to confession for years. Every time his wife urged him to go, he would beat her. A priest told her to give the husband a little picture of the Immaculate Conception. Immediately after he received the picture he had a desire to go to confession. He went the following morning, telling the priest that it had been twenty-eight years since he had gone to confession, but after receiving the picture of the Immaculate Conception he suddenly wanted to go. He said that last night every minute seemed like a thousand years.

The holiness of Mary, free from all sin is a model for all of us. We are encouraged to intercede through her that we may grow in holiness and be more pleasing to God who gave us life.

In his apostolic constitution *Ineffabilis Deus*, promulgated on December 8, 1854, Pope Pius IX declared that it was now a dogma of the Church that Mary was conceived without sin. He said: *Indeed it was wholly fitting that so wonderful a mother should be ever resplendent with glory of most sublime holiness and so completely free from all taint of original sin that she would triumph utterly over the ancient serpent . . . .* Whatever honor and praise are bestowed on the Mother redound to the Son.

Pope Pius IX says: *We declare, pronounce, and define that the doctrine which holds that the most Blessed Virgin Mary, in the first instant of her conception, by a singular grace and privilege granted by Almighty God, in view of the merits of Jesus Christ, the Savior of the human race, was preserved free from all stain of original sin, is a doctrine revealed by God and therefore to be believed firmly and constantly by all the faithful.*

We are all called to be saints. It should not be the unusual, but the usual. We learn in the most basic of catechisms that the reason we were created by God is to know, love and serve him here on earth, and after, to see and enjoy him for ever in heaven. In his great novel, *The Woman Who Was Poor*, Leon Bloy, said it all when he stated that the only tragedy is not to be a saint!

Our Lady does not want that tragedy to happen to any one of us. No matter how far away one is from God, Mary, his Mother, is there to bring the sinner back. All one has to do is to ask her help and she takes one's hand and leads the way.

St Anthony of Padua (1193-1231) composed a beautiful prayer to Mary:

O Sweet name, which gives the sinner strength and the blessed hope. We pray to you, our Lady, Star of the Sea. Shine upon us in our distress on the sea of life, and lead us to safe harbor and the ineffable joys of eternity.

We spend so much of our lives "getting and spending" worldly things and put our spiritual welfare way far down on our list of importance. Certainly God wants us to take our earthly vocation seriously and have a responsibility for the operation of the world. Doing all things for God makes our whole life a prayer. Mary can help us to put first things first and then all the pieces of our life's puzzle fit perfectly, and despite set backs and problems we are happy. We must let Christ help us to carry our crosses. Then we will realize that the greatest responsibility we have to our neighbor is to bring him or her to Christ so that he or she can know God here and be with him for ever in heaven.

The Assumption of Our Lady

Some say that Our Lady "died" in Ephesus and it was from there she was taken up to heaven. But others maintain that it was in Jerusalem that she came to the end of her earthly life. There on Mount Sion, close to the Cenacle, where Christ instituted the Holy Eucharist, Mary lived after the death of her Son. This is according to an ancient tradition, which also says that the area was where the first Christian community lived. This area eventually became the place where the Basilica of Sion was built. In the war of 1948 the whole area was badly bombed and eventually was taken over by the Jewish State. However, there is a church close by called the Church of the Domition. In the crypt there is a beautiful statue of the Virgin, which lies in the slumber of a peaceful death.

We know that Mary is truly the Mother of the Holy Eucharist. The Son of God would not subsist in the Eucharist if he had not first become flesh in the womb of Our Lady.

When Mary conceived Jesus, Our Lord, she went joyfully on a three-days journey to help her cousin Elizabeth. She actually took Jesus to her. So also should we, when we receive Jesus in Holy

Communion, take him to our brothers and sisters, to our homes, to our places of work, to the countryside and the cities, to the whole world!

In the *Catechism of the Catholic Church* we read, #s 965/906; *After her Son's Ascension, Mary 'aided the beginnings of the Church by her prayers.' (Lumen Gentium #69) In her association with the apostles and several women, 'we also see Mary by her prayers imploring the gift of the Spirit, who had already overshadowed her in the Annunciation.'* (Ibid #59)

'Finally the Immaculate Virgin, preserved free from all stain of sin, when the course of her earthly life was finished, was taken up body and soul into heavenly glory, and exalted by the Lord as Queen over all things, so that she might be more fully conformed to her Son, the Lord of lords and conqueror of sin and death.' (Ibid #59) *The Assumption of the Blessed Virgin is a singular participation in her Son's Resurrection and an anticipation of the resurrection of other Christians.*

The Catechism goes on to quote from the Byzantine Liturgy for the feast of the Dormition of Our Lady: *In giving birth you kept your virginity, in your Dormition you did not leave the world, O Mother of God, but were joined to the Source of Life. You conceived the living God and, by your prayers, will deliver our souls from death.*

On November 1, 1950, Pope Pius XII defined the dogma of the Assumption. He solemnly proclaimed that the belief that Mary, at the end of her earthly life, was taken body and soul, into heaven, was part of the deposit of faith, given to us by the apostles. The Assumption confirms us in the virtue of hope that we too, after our life on earth, being faithful to God's will, shall rise from the dead on the last day, when our bodies will be united to our souls, to enjoy the beauty of God forever.

In one of the opening prayers in the Mass of the Assumption a phrase from the Book of Revelation is used: *This woman clothed with the sun,* we ask Our Lady *to bring Jesus to the waiting world and fill the void of incompletion with the presence of her child.* The Church tells us that Mary is now in the presence of God the Father, since she was assumed into heaven, body and soul and raised to be Queen of all creation.

In the preface of the Mass we read: *Today the Virgin Mother of God was taken up into heaven to be the beginning and pattern of the Church in its perfection, and a sign of hope and comfort for your people on their pilgrim way.*

Mary as Co-Redemptrix

Quoting *Lumen Gentium* (#62) the *Catechism of the Catholic Church* says: *This motherhood of Mary in the order of grace continues uninteruptedly from the consent which she loyally gave at the Annunciation and which she sustained without wavering beneath the cross, until the eternal fulfilment of all the elect. Taken up to heaven she did not lay aside this saving office, but by her manifold intercession continues to bring us the gift of eternal salvation.... Therefore the Blessed Virgin is invoked in the Church under titles of Advocate, Helper, Benefactress and Mediatrix.*

So we have Our Blessed Mother ever ready to help us grow in our spiritual life and bring us closer to Christ. Her great desire is to bring all of mankind to God. It is commonly held by theologians that a true devotion to Mary is one of the signs of predestination. There never was a saint who did not have great love for Our Lady. The great spiritual writer Fr Garrigou-Lagrange tells us that Mary is not the Mother of all in a general way as we might think of Eve in the natural order, but the mother of each person in particular, for she intercedes for each and obtains for each all the graces one receives.

St. Pope Pius X said: *God could have given us the Redeemer of the human race, and the Founder of the Faith in a way other than through the Virgin, but since Divine Providence has been pleased that we should have the God-man through Mary, who conceived him by the Holy Spirit and bore him in her womb, it only remains for us to receive Christ from the hands of Mary.*

It's as if Mary is the bridge between man and her Son Jesus. St Bernard, like so many great saints has said God wills that we should have nothing that has not passed through the hands of Mary. Again Fr Garrigou-Lagrange, talking about our great prayer, the Hail Mary, which we say so many times each day, says that in the prayer we pray for grace when we say *pray for us sinners, now and at the hour of our death.* When we use the word *now* we ask for the grace necessary to fulfill our duty of the present moment, in order to practice a particular virtue asked of us here and now. And we ask for the grace in order to die a holy and happy death.

How true it is that if we think of our last end we will not sin, because our last end - our death - is the beginning of our forever. It is for what we were born and for what we live our whole lives - to arrive at our heavenly home and there be greeted by God the Father, God the Son and God the Holy Spirit; and the Blessed Mother of God.

St Alphonsus Liguori tells us: *Jesus is the only Mediator of justice, and that by his merits he obtained for us all graces and salvation; but Mary is the mediatrix of grace, because she prays and asks for it in the name of Jesus.* Mary continues to act as she did when she lived after her Son's death. Her vocation in the Church was different from that of St Peter. She had no role of ruling the Church. Hers was the quiet vocation of contemplation, much like that of the men and women who play out their lives in contemplative religious orders. She continues to pray for the Church and for all of us, her children.

When writing about Our Lady as the Mediatrix of all graces, the Official Handbook of the Legion of Mary, presents it in a most clear and simple paragraph:

By the ordinance of God, Mary's power is without limit. All that he could give her, he has given to her. All that she was capable of receiving, she received in plenitude. For us God has constituted her a special means of grace. Operating in union with her we approach him more effectively, and hence win grace more fully. Indeed we place ourselves in the very flood-tide of grace, for she is the spouse of the Holy Spirit. She is the channel of every grace which Jesus Christ has won. We receive nothing which we do not owe to a positive intervention on her part. She does not content herself with transmitting all: She obtains all for us.

Since we all experience sorrow we are able to appreciate the sorrow Our Lady suffered throughout her life. If we experience great sorrow we will be able to really appreciate the great sorrow of Mary Our Mother. From the very beginning of our introduction to Our Lady in the gospel we realize that her life was not easy. There is the misunderstanding when she is found with child. Joseph wanted to put her away quietly, but she does not reveal the mystery of her pregnancy. It is the angel who tells Joseph.

She must go to Bethlehem to fulfill the law, just as she is about to give birth to Jesus. In her circumstances, even today, the journey from Nazareth to Bethlehem would not be easy. Then there was the flight into Egypt to save the life of the infant Jesus and their time in a strange country.

When Mary was told that a sword would pierce her heart, she knew quite well of that sorrow. Our Lord told St Catherine of Siena that from the moment his Mother said yes to the Angel Gabriel, her cooperation in his life and passion began; She became the Co-Redemptrix. In modern times, on April 25, 1942, Christ told Bethe Petit a holy lady from Belgium that by her acceptance of Calvary his Mother participated in all his sufferings. He said: *Devotion to her heart united to mine will bring peace, that true peace, so often implored and yet so little merited.*

St. Thomas Aquinas has written: *Christ alone is the perfect mediator between God and man . . . . but there is nothing to prevent others, in a certain way, from being called mediators between God and man in so far as they, by preparing or serving, cooperate in uniting man to God. (Summa Theologiae, III, Q-26, a) Mary is the one who more than all the angels and all creatures cooperates with God in bringing all creation to him.*

When I first visited the beautiful Basilica of Our Lady of the Immaculate Conception in Washington DC, I was thrilled to see that there were three niches to the left of the high altar, two of which were backed by magnificent mosaics, one of Our Lady of the Immaculate Conception and the other of Our Lady of the Assumption. I wondered then if the third which had no mosaic was waiting for Our Lady Co-Redemptrix. Last year I noticed that the niche is still waiting for a mosaic.

In the Glories of Mary, St Alphonsus quoting Suarez writes: *The Most Holy Virgin had more faith than all men and angels. She saw her Son in the crib of Bethlehem, and believed him to be the creator of the world. She saw him fly from Herod, and still believed him to be the King of kings. She saw him born, and believed him to be eternal. She saw him poor and hungry, and believed him to be the Lord of the universe. She saw him lying on straw, and believed him to be omnipotent. She observed that he did not speak, and believed him infinite wisdom. She heard him weep, and believed him the joy of paradise. In fine, she saw him in death, despised and crucified, and, although faith wavered in others, Mary remained firm in the belief that he was God.*

There was no doubt in her mind that her Son was not God. She knew that the baby she was carrying in her womb was God and the child she nursed was

God and the boy who she thought was lost was God. She knew that the young man who went about Galilee doing good was God and she knew that when she asked him to help the young married couple in Cana that he would, because he could do all things - he was God.

Our Lady appeared to St Mechtilda and told her that the Holy Spirit had showered her with so many graces that she was able to give these graces in abundance to those who ask for them through her as Mediatrix.

And Fr Garrigou-Lagrange, the great Dominican theologian writes in his wonderful book *The Mother of the Savior: Mary's universal mediation appears to be capable of definition as a dogma of faith; it is at least implicitly revealed and it is already universally proposed by the ordinary magisterium of the Church.* I believe that we are very much in the age of Mary and perhaps I will see that third mosaic installed in Washington, and it will be that of Our Lady Co-Redemptrix.

The Sorrowful and Immaculate Heart of Mary

In his encyclical *Monse Maio* of April 30, 1965, on the devotion to Mary during the month of

May, Pope Paul VI speaking about the present need of the Church and the world wrote: *We have compelling reasons for believing that the present hour is especially grave; that it makes a call for united prayer from the whole Christian people more than ever a matter of urgency.* He ended the encyclical saying: *Do not fail to lay careful stress on the saying of the Rosary, the prayer so dear to Our Lady and so highly recommended by the Supreme Pontiffs.* In the more than thirty years since that encyclical was written, things have not improved in the Church or in the world. We need to pray harder. However, we must be optimistic, because there are many people praying, as Our Lady has been asking through time.

Devotion to the Sorrowful and Immaculate Heart of Mary, a devotion beloved by her Son, has been gaining in recent years. Apart from the feast which is celebrated the day after the feast of the Sacred Heart, every First Saturday of the year is another day to advance this devotion. In order to make the world more conscious of God we need to advance his causes. He wants the best for all, but so many have turned their backs on him. Hearts need to be charged.

Berthe Petit, whom we mentioned before tells us that Our Lord appeared to her on July 2, 1940, and told her: *It is hearts that must be changed. This will be accomplished only by the devotion proclaimed, explained, preached and recommended everywhere. Recourse to my Mother under the title (Sorrowful and Immaculate Heart of Mary) I wish for her universally, is the last help I shall give before the end of time.*

Fr Garrigou-Lagrange thought very highly of Berthe Petit whom he met in Switzerland during the First World War. He also had a great fondness for this devotion. In a brief appreciation of Berthe Petit he wrote: *When we say 'Immaculate Heart of Mary,' we recall what she received from God in the first instant of her conception. When we say 'Sorrowful Heart,' we recall all that Mary has suffered and offered for us in union with her Son, from the words of holy Simeon to Calvary, and until her holy death.*

The devotion is by no way a new one. It goes back to the 17 century when St John Eudes (1601 - 1680) preached it together with devotion to the Sacred Heart of Jesus. He believed that both devotions go hand in hand.

This was verified almost two hundred years later when Our Lady made the miraculous medal known to St Catherine Labouré in 1830 at the convent in Rue du Bac, Paris. And it took almost another hundred years when the message of the suffering and Immaculate Heart of Mary would be brought to the faithful through the visits Our Lady made to Fatima in 1917.

It has always been the same message which Our Lady brings to the world - pray and do penance. The power of prayer is so well known and has proven over and over again that it is the answer to all our problems. While the sacrifice of the Mass is the greatest form of worship and it should be the center of our lives, the Holy Rosary has been given to us as an ideal prayer, where we meditate on the life of Christ and his Mother. It is a prayer which may be said anywhere and at any time. The power of even one Hail Mary is so great, that we should make, at least one part of the Rosary a daily exercise.

Writing about the Hail Mary in the *Secret of the Rosary*, St Louis de Montfort says, *Although this new hymn (Hail Mary) is in praise of the Mother of God and is sung directly to her, nevertheless it greatly glorifies the Most Blessed Trinity because any homage that we pay Our Lady returns to God who is the cause of all her virtues and perfections. When we honor Our Lady; God the Father is glorified because we are honoring the most perfect of his creatures;*

God the Son is glorified because we are praising his most pure Mother; and God the Holy Spirit is glorified because we are lost in admiration at the graces with which he has filled his spouse.

It is interesting to note that the Mass for the feast of the Immaculate Heart of Mary was made an obligatory memorial (a universal Mass) as late as last year by Pope John Paul II. We are certainly in the age of Mary. All generations will call her blessed, but we have come to the time when more voices will be raised to call her blessed!

2

Marian Prayers

The Hail Mary
Hail Mary, full of grace, the Lord is with thee; Blessed art thou among women, and blessed is the fruit of thy womb, Jesus.

Holy Mary, Mother of God, pray for us sinners, now and at the hour of our death. Amen.

Morning Offering
O Jesus, through the most pure Heart of Mary, I offer all my thoughts, works, actions, prayers, joys and sufferings of this day for the intentions of your Sacred Heart. I offer them especially for the Holy Souls in Purgatory. Amen.

Hail Holy Queen
Hail, Holy Queen, Mother of Mercy.
Hail our life, our sweetness and our hope!

*To you do we cry, poor banished children of Eve!
To you do we send up our sighs; mourning and
weeping in this vale of tears!
Turn then, most gracious Advocate, your eyes of
mercy toward us; and after this, our exile, show unto
us the blessed fruit of your womb, Jesus!
O clement, O loving, O sweet Virgin Mary!*

The Memorare

This wonderful prayer to Our Lady is said to have been composed by St Bernard, who had a great devotion to Mary, true Mother of God.

*Remember, O most gracious Virgin Mary that never was it known that anyone who fled to your protection, implored your help, or sought your intercession was left unaided.
Inspired with this confidence, I fly to you O Virgin of virgins, my mother. To you I come, before you I stand, sinful and sorrowful.
O Mother of the Word Incarnate, despise not my petitions, but in your mercy, hear and answer me.
Amen.*

The Angelus

V. The Angel of the Lord declared unto Mary,
R. And She conceived of the Holy Spirit.
>*Hail Mary, etc.*

V. Behold the handmaid of the Lord,
R. Be it done unto me according to your Word.
>*Hail Mary, etc.*

V. And the Word was made flesh
R. And dwelt among us.
>*Hail Mary, etc.*

V. Pray for us, O holy Mother of God.
R. That we may be made worthy of the promises of Christ.

Let us pray:
Pour forth, we beseech you, O Lord, your grace into our hearts; that we to whom the incarnation of Christ, your Son, was made known by the message of an angel, may by his passion and cross be brought to the glory of his resurrection, through the same Christ our Lord. Amen.

Regina Caeli

V. *Queen of heaven, rejoice! Alleluia.*
R. *For he whom you did merit to bear. Alleluia.*

V. *Has risen, as he said. Alleluia.*
R. *Pray for us to God. Alleluia.*

V. *Rejoice and be glad, O Virgin Mary. Alleluia.*
R. *For the Lord is truly risen. Alleluia.*

Let us pray:
O God, who gave joy to the world through the resurrection of your Son, our Lord Jesus Christ, grant we beseech you, that through the intercession of the Virgin Mary, his Mother, we may obtain the joys of everlasting life, through the same Christ our Lord. Amen.

The Holy Rosary

The Holy Rosary is a formula of prayer, made up of 15 decades of *Hail Marys*, with an *Our Father* said before each decade and a *Glory Be to the Father* at the end of each decade. The recitation of each decade is accompanied by a pious meditation on a particular mystery of our Redemption—from the lives of Our Lord and his Blessed Mother.

The 15 mysteries to be meditated are:

Joyful
(Mondays and Thursdays)
1. The Annunciation
2. The Visitation
3. The Birth of Our Lord
4. The Presentation of Christ in the Temple
5. The Finding of the Child Jesus in the Temple

Sorrowful
(Tuesdays and Fridays)
1. The Agony in the Garden
2. The Scourging at the Pillar
3. The Crowning with Thorns
4. The Carrying of the Cross
5. The Crucifixion and Death of Our Lord

Glorious
(Wednesdays, Saturdays and Sundays)
1. The Resurrection of Our Lord
2. The Ascension of Our Lord

3. The Descent of the Holy Spirit on the Apostles
4. The Assumption of Our Lady into Heaven
5. The Coronation of Our Lady

The Litany of Our Lady

Lord, have mercy on us.
Christ, have mercy on us.

Lord, have mercy on us. Christ, hear us.
Christ, graciously hear us.

God the Father of heaven, have mercy on us.
God the Son, redeemer of the world, have mercy on us.
God the Holy Spirit, have mercy on us.
Holy Trinity, one God, have mercy on us.

Holy Mary,	*pray for us*
Holy Mother of God,	*pray for us*
Holy Virgin of virgins,	*pray for us*
Mother of Christ,	*pray for us*
Mother of the Church,	*pray for us*
Mother of divine grace,	*pray for us*
Mother most pure,	*pray for us*

Mother most chaste,   *pray for us*
Mother inviolate,   *pray for us*
Mother undefiled,   *pray for us*
Mother most amiable,   *pray for us*
Mother most admirable,   *pray for us*
Mother of good council,   *pray for us*
Mother of our Creator,   *pray for us*
Mother of our Savior,   *pray for us*
Virgin most prudent,   *pray for us*
Virgin most venerable,   *pray for us*
Virgin most renowned,   *pray for us*
Virgin most powerful,   *pray for us*
Virgin most merciful,   *pray for us*
Virgin most faithful,   *pray for us*
Mirror of justice,   *pray for us*
Seat of wisdom,   *pray for us*
Cause of our joy,   *pray for us*
Spiritual vessel,   *pray for us*
Vessel of honor,   *pray for us*
Singular vessel of devotion,   *pray for us*
Mystical rose,   *pray for us*
Tower of David,   *pray for us*
Tower of ivory,   *pray for us*
House of gold,   *pray for us*
Ark of the covenant,   *pray for us*

Gate of heaven,	*pray for us*
Morning star,	*pray for us*
Health of the sick,	*pray for us*
Refuge of sinners,	*pray for us*
Comforter of the afflicted,	*pray for us*
Help of Christians,	*pray for us*
Queen of angels,	*pray for us*
Queen of patriarchs,	*pray for us*
Queen of prophets,	*pray for us*
Queen of apostles,	*pray for us*
Queen of martyrs,	*pray for us*
Queen of confessors,	*pray for us*
Queen of virgins,	*pray for us*
Queen of all saints,	*pray for us*
Queen conceived without original sin	*pray for us*
Queen assumed into heaven,	*pray for us*
Queen of the most holy Rosary,	*pray for us*
Queen of peace,	*pray for us*

V.   *Lamb of God who takes away the sins of the world,*
R.   *Spare us, O Lord.*
V.   *Lamb of God who takes away the sins of the world,*
R.   *Graciously hear us, O Lord.*

V.   *Lamb of God who takes away the sins of the world,*
R.   *Have mercy on us.*
V.   *Pray for us, O holy Mother of God.*
R.   *That we may be made worthy of the promises of Christ.*

Let us pray:
O God, whose only begotten Son, by his life, death, and resurrection, has purchased for us the rewards of everlasting life; grant, we beseech you, that we who meditate upon these mysteries of the most holy rosary of the Blessed Virgin Mary, may both imitate what they contain, and attain to what they promise. We ask this through Christ our Lord. Amen

Prayer to Mary—After Communion

Mary, holy Virgin Mother,
I have received your Son, Jesus Christ.
With love you became his Mother,
gave birth to him, nursed him,
and helped him grow to manhood.
With love I return him to you,
to hold once more,
to love with all your heart,

*and to offer to the Holy Trinity
as our supreme act of worship
for your honor and for the good
of all your pilgrim brothers and sisters.*

*Mother, ask God to forgive my sins and to help me serve him more faithfully.
Keep me true to Christ until death,
and let me come to praise him with you for ever and ever. Amen.*

Consecration to Our Lady

O hail Mary, my Mother and my Queen, into your blessed trust and loving care, and into the heart of your mercy, I this day, and every day, and at the hour of my death, commend my whole self.

Into your hands I place all my hope and happiness, all my cares and concerns and my whole life, that, through your most holy intercession and through your merits, all my actions may be guided and directed according to your will and that of your divine Son. Amen.

Our Lady Refuge of Sinners

Almighty and merciful God, who did appoint the Blessed, ever Virgin Mary to be the refuge of sinners, grant that under her protection we may be delivered from all guilt, and obtain the happiness which your mercy brings, through Christ our Lord. Amen.

Our Lady of Perpetual Help

O Mother of Perpetual Help, behold at your feet a wretched sinner who turns to you and puts his trust in you. Mother of mercy, have pity on me. I hear all call you the refuge and hope of sinners: be then my refuge and my hope. Help me for the love of Jesus Christ; hold out your hand to a fallen wretch who commends himself to you and dedicates himself for ever to your service. Praise and thanks be to God, who in his great mercy has given me this trust in you, sure pledge of my eternal salvation.

It is but too true that in the past I have fallen miserably, because I did not turn to you. I know that with your help I shall conquer; I know you will keep me, if I commend myself to you; but I fear that in the occasions of sin I may forget to call upon you and so be lost. This, then, is the grace I ask of you with all my heart and soul; that in the assaults of hell I may ever run to your protection and say to you: Help me, Mary; Mother of Perpetual Help, let me not lose my God. Amen.

Our Lady of Good Counsel

Most glorious Virgin, chosen by the eternal Wisdom to be the Mother of the eternal Word in the flesh, you who are the treasure of God's graces and the advocate of sinners, I your most unworthy servant turn to you; be pleased to guide and counsel me in this vale of trees.

Obtain for me, through the precious Blood of your divine Son, the forgiveness of my sins, the salvation of my soul, and the means necessary to bring it about.

Obtain also for holy Church victory over her enemies and the spread of the Kingdom of Jesus Christ over the whole earth. Amen.

Our Lady of Knock

Our Lady of Knock, Queen of Ireland, you gave hope to your people in a time of distress, and comforted them in sorrow. You have inspired countless pilgrims to pray with confidence to your Divine Son, remembering his promise 'Ask and you shall receive, seek and you shall find.'

Help me to remember that we are all pilgrims on the road to heaven. Fill me with love and concern for my brothers and sisters in Christ, especially those who live with me. Comfort me when I am sick, or lonely or depressed. Teach me how to take part ever more reverently in the Holy Mass. Pray for me now, and at the hour of my death. Amen.

3

Prayers of the Saints and Holy People to the Blessed Virgin

Many more prayers to Our Lady composed by the saints and other holy people throughout the years could have been included. This is simply a small example.

Prayer of St Ephraem
(Circa 306-373)

O pure, spotless, and blessed Virgin, sinless Mother of your mighty Son, the Lord of the universe, you who are inviolate and most holy, the hope of those who are guilty beyond hope, we sing your praise. You who are full of every grace, who gave birth to Christ the God-man, we bless you, we all bow low before you, all invoke you and implore your aid. Virgin holy and undefiled, rescue us from all cruel pressure and all temptations of the devil.

Be our intercessor and advocate at the hour of death and judgement; deliver us from the time that is never guarded from the outer darkness; make us worthy to share the glory of your Son, O dearest and most gentle Virgin Mother. You are indeed our only hope, a hope most sure and sacred in the sight of God. To him be honor and glory, majesty and dominion, for ever and ever, world without end. Amen.

Prayer of St Germanus of Constantinople
(d. 448)

O Mary, by your pure and Immaculate Conception make my body pure and my soul holy. Amen.

Prayer of St John Damascene
(690-749)

Having confidence in you, O Mother of God, I shall be saved. Being under your protection, I shall fear nothing. With your help, I shall give battle to my enemies and put them to flight; for devotion to you is an arm of salvation. Amen.

Prayer of St Pascahasius
(d. 860)

Deign, O Immaculate Virgin, Mother most pure, to accept the loving cry of praise which we send up to you from the depths of our hearts. Though they can but add little to your glory, O Queen of Angels, you do not despise, in your love, the praises of the humble and the poor.

Cast down upon us a glance of mercy, O most glorious Queen; graciously receive our petitions. Through your immaculate purity of body and mind, which rendered you so pleasing to God, inspire us with a love of innocence and purity.

Teach us to guard carefully the gifts of grace, striving ever after sanctity, so that, being made like the image of your beauty, we may be worthy to become the sharers of thy eternal happiness. Amen.

Prayer of St Anselm
(1033-1109)

Dearest Virgin, by the merits of your saving annunciation and by the angelical greeting which you received from holy Gabriel, the messenger of Salvation, messenger of the Incarnation of God's Word, messenger of life everlasting and our salvation through you, I pray you to receive our prayers. All-merciful Lady, great are my sins, but greater is your grace, for you are full of grace, and the Lord is with you; blessed are you among women, and blessed is the fruit of your womb

Mother of all grace, pray for me. With your annunciation the reign of original sin draw near to its end, and hope dawned, for to all who in truth awaited it, your annunciation was the fount and channel of grace to come.

When I call it to mind, and dwell on it in my thoughts, and with my lips gave honor to that joy of your, let that remembrance be the end and abolution of all my guilt, past and present; let it bring me saving grace and lasting purity of heart. Help me, Lady, hope of the living and comfort of those who mourn, support of those in need and compassionate friend of all, so that I who by the very bitterness of my grief, and by the sore weakness with which I am stricken, recognize my guilt, may through the joys of your holy annunciation have my sickness healed and by your mercy feel my sorrow turned to joy.

Then let me learn to please God in future by grieving where grief will not be thrown away, by purity of body and soul, by humility of heart, by fulness of faith, and by all goodness.

Let my spirit exalt in God my Savior every moment of my life. Holy Mother of God, help me, plead for me, sinner that I am, with your beloved Son. Amen.

Prayer of St Bernard
(1090-1153)

O Mary, our hope, hear this prayer. Illumine our path, O Star of the Sea, shine on us buffeted by storms; guide us to the harbor at the hour of our death, comfort us with your protecting presence, so that without fear we may arrive at our eternal home in happiness. Amen.

Prayer of St Anthony of Padua
(1195-1231)

O Lady, our hope, hear our prayer. You who are the Star of the Sea, shine on us, tormented as we are by storms! Let your presence comfort us at the moment of death so that without fear we can look forward to the indescribable joys of heaven.

Prayer of St Gertrude
(1236-1301)

I praise you, most compassionate Jesus, through your own sweet Heart, for that most ardent mutual love which united your divine heart to that of the Virgin undefiled, and which most intimately and inseparately united your glorious divinity with your humanity in her chaste womb. Thus was it given her to imitate you in the greatness of your love; you, Life of all that lives, who in your boundless love suffered a cruel death on the cross to redeem mankind.

I praise you and greet you, Mother of graces, worthiest shrine of the Holy Spirit, by the sweet Heart of Jesus, the Son of God the Father, and your child. And I entreat you to come to our help in every need, and at the hour of our death. Amen.

Prayer of St Gertrude

Hail Mary, queen of mercy, olive branch of forgiveness, through whom we receive the medicine that heals our mortal sickness, the balsam of pardon; Virgin Mother of the divine offspring, through whom the grace of heavenly light has been shed upon us, the sweet-scented descendant son of Israel! Through your Son, your only Child who stooped to become the

Brother of mankind, you are the true Mother of us all. For the sake of his love take me, all unworthy as I am, into your motherly care. Sustain, preserve, and enlighten my conversion; be for all eternity my incomparable cherished Mother, tenderly caring for me throughout my earthly life, and enfolding me in your arms at the hour of my death. Amen.

Prayer of St Catherine of Siena
(1347-1380)

O Mary, you bring us the fire of God's mercy! You are the liberator of the human race, since Christ purchased it with his passion, and you Mother, purchased it with the pain of your body and the anguish of your soul. Amen.

Prayer of St John of the Cross
(1542-1591)

Most holy Mary, Virgin of virgins, shrine of the most Holy Trinity, joy of the angels, sure refuge of sinners, take pity on our sorrows, mercifully accept our sighs, and appease the wrath of your most holy Son. Amen.

Prayer of St Aloysius Gonzaga
(1568-1591)

O Holy Mary! my Mother; into your blessed trust and special custody, and into the bosom of your mercy, this day and every day and at the hour of my death, I commend my soul and body. To you I commit all my worries and sorrows, my life and the end of it, that by your most holy intercession, and by your merits, all my actions may be directed and governed by your will and that of your Son. Amen.

Consecration of St. Louis de Montfort
(1673-1716)

I salute you, O Immaculate Mary, loving tabernacle of the Divinity! I salute you, O sure refuge of sinners! Hear the desires which I have of the Divine Wisdom, and for that end receive the vows and offerings which my lowness presents to you . . . . In the presence of all the heavenly court I choose you this day for my Mother and Mistress. I deliver and consecrate to you, as your slave, my body and soul, my goods, both interior and exterior, and even the value of all my good actions, past, present and future, leaving to you the entire and full right of disposing of me and all that belongs to me, according to your good pleasure, to the greatest glory of God, in time and eternity. Amen.

Prayer of St Dominic Savio
(1842 1857)

O Mary, I wish always to be your child. I give you my heart; keep it for ever.

O Jesus, O Mary, be always my friends. I pray you both to let me die rather than commit a sin. Amen.

Prayer of St John Bosco
(1815-1888)

O Mary, powerful Virgin, you mighty and glorious protector of holy Church; you marvelous help of Christians; you who are awe-inspiring as an army in battle array; you by whom alone all heresies throughout the world are brought to nothing: in our anguish, our struggles, our distress, guard us from the enemy's power, and at the hour of our death bid our souls welcome into paradise. Amen.

Consecration composed by Berthe Petit
(1870-1943)

Sorrowful and Immaculate Heart of Mary, dwelling pure and holy, cover my soul with your maternal protection so that being faithful to the voice of Jesus, it responds to his love and obeys his Divine will.

I wish, O, my Mother, to keep unceasingly before me your co-redemption in order to live intimately with your heart that is totally united to the Heart of your Divine Son.

Fasten me to his heart by your own virtue and sorrows. Protect me always. Amen.

Blessed Miguel Pro
(1891-1927)

Let me live my life at your side, my Mother, and be the companion of your bitter solitude and your profound pain. Let my soul feel your eyes' sad weeping and the abandonment of your heart.

On the road of my life, I do not wish to savor the happiness of Bethlehem, adoring the Child Jesus in your virginal arms. I do not wish to enjoy the amiable presence of Jesus Christ in the humble little house of Nazareth. I do not care to accompany you on your glorious Assumption to the angels' choir.

For my life, I covet the years and mockery of Calvary; the slow agony of your Son, the contempt, the ignominy, the infamy of his cross. I wish to stand at your side, most sorrowful virgin, strengthening my spirit with your tears, consummating my sacrifice with your martyrdom, sustaining my heart with your solitude, loving my God and your God with the immolation of my being. Amen.

Prayer of Pope John Paul II

O Immaculate Virgin, Mother of the true God and Mother of the Church! You, who from this place revealed your clemency and your pity to all those who asked for your protection; hear the prayer that we address to you with filial trust, and present it to your Son Jesus, our sole Redeemer.

Mother of mercy, Teacher of hidden and silent sacrifice, to you, who come to meet us sinners, we dedicate on this day all our being and all our love. We also dedicate to you our life, our work, our joys, our infirmities, and our sorrows.

Grant peace, justice and prosperity to our peoples; for we entrust to your care all that we have and all that we are, our Lady and Mother.

We wish to be entirely yours and to walk with you along the way of complete faithfulness to Jesus Christ in His Church: hold us always with loving hands.

Virgin of Guadalupe, Mother of the Americas, we pray to you for all the bishops, that they may lead the faithful along paths of intense Christian life, of love and humble service of God and souls.

Contemplate the immense harvest, and intercede with the Lord that he may instill a hunger for holiness in the whole People of God, and grant abundant vocations of priests and religious, strong in the faith and zealous dispensers of God's mysteries.

Grant to our homes the grace of loving and respecting life in its beginnings, with the same love with which you conceived in your womb the life of the Son of God. Blessed Virgin Mary, Mother of fair love, protect our families, so that they may always be united, and bless the upbringing of our children.

Our hope, look upon us with compassion, teach us to go continually to Jesus and, if we fall, help us to rise again, to return to him, by means of confession of our faults and sins in the Sacrament of Penance, which gives peace to the soul. We beg you to grant us a great love for all the Sacraments, which are, as it were, the signs that your Son left us on earth.

Thus, Most Holy Mother, with the peace of God in our conscience, with our hearts free from evil and hatred, we will be able to bring to all true joy and true peace, which comes to us from your Son, our Lord Jesus Christ, who with the Father and the Holy Spirit, lives and reigns for ever and ever. Amen.

4

Feasts of Our Lady

We Catholics start off the year - January 1 - with the feast day of Mary, Mother of God. She is our mother too; the Mother of God is our mother! It is fitting that such should be the feast on the first day of the year. It is her greatest title and for us it points out her great power as our greatest intercessor with her Son, God the Second Person of the Holy Trinity.

But as Catholics our Liturgical year starts with the First Sunday in Advent and within a few days we celebrate the feast of the Immaculate Conception on December 8. This feast of Our Lady had been celebrated from early times both in the East and West. When Pope Pius IX proclaimed the dogma that Mary was conceived without the stain of original sin, on December 8, 1854, he was affirming the constant faith of the Church. Mary's total freedom from sin, from her conception, is the result of her Son's Redemption which in time was to come after this great grace given to Mary who from all eternity was chosen to be the Mother of God.

In the entrance antiphon of the Mass for this feast day we say with Mary: *I exalt for joy in the Lord, my soul rejoices in my God; for he has clothed me in the garment of salvation and robed me in the cloak of justice, like a bride adorned with her jewels.* (Is 61 10)

On December 12 we celebrate the feast of Our Lady of Guadalupe. At first Our Lady under this title was chosen as the Patroness of Mexico, where true devotion seems to be in the blood of every Mexican. Later Our Lady has been called Patroness of the Americas under this title and justifiably so. Over the gifts the priest says: *grant that this sacrifice will strengthen us to fulfill your commandments as true sons and daughters of the Virgin Mary.*

In less than two weeks we again celebrate a great feast of Mary - the Birth of the Son of God and her Son in Bethlehem. While the day first of all belongs to Jesus, we find Mary very much there. As in all her feasts she wants us to find her Son and fall in love with him. We can say with Mary in the responsorial psalm: *Forever I will sing the goodness of the Lord.*

We have already mentioned January 1, the feast of Mary, Mother of God. In the alternative opening prayer we say, *the Virgin conceived and bore your Son, who is called Wonderful God, Prince of Peace. May her prayer, the gift of a mother's love, be your people's joy through all ages.*

On February 2, we celebrate the Presentation of the Lord in the Temple. While once again this is primarily the feast of Christ, we again see Our Blessed Mother presenting her Son to the priest of the temple and afterwards to Simeon and Anna. Since we are all human we share the same blood and flesh; and since Christ is human he shares our blood and flesh in the same way (see Heb 2 14). However, in a more real way the Blood and Flesh of Christ have been taken from his Mother Mary. Her blood will flow when her Son's falls on the earth on Good Friday.

On February 11 the Mass commemorates the apparition of Mary in 1858 to St Bernadette, where Our Lady said to the little girl: *I am the Immaculate Conception*, confirming the dogma proclaimed by Pope Pius IX four years before. In the responsorial psalm we cry out: *You are the highest honor of our race!*

The greatest of Mary's feast days is on March 25 - the Annunciation. The day our God was made flesh. It was on this day that Mary said yes to the will of God and set in motion our salvation. In the opening prayer we say: *God, our Father, your Word became man and was born of the Virgin Mary. May we become more like Jesus Christ, whom we acknowledge as our redeemer, God and man.* Mary possesses the Son of God in her womb. She is truly the Mother of God and our Mother too.

On May 13 we have the feast of Our Lady of Fatima. The Mass said on this day is the common of the Blessed Virgin Mary in which we say the entrance antiphon, *Hail, holy Mother! The child to whom you gave birth is the King of heaven and earth for ever.* The opening prayer of this mass contains the following: *Lord God, give to your people the joy of continued health in mind and body. With the prayers of the Virgin Mary to help us, guide us through the sorrows of this life to eternal happiness in the life to come.*

May 31 is another beautiful feast of Mary. It commemorates the visit she paid to her cousin Elizabeth, and shows the great human kindness of Our Lady. She went a journey of three days to be of service to her cousin and remained with her for three months until Elizabeth's son, St John the Baptist, was born. In the Alleluia of the Mass we hear St Elizabeth, inspired by God, say: *Blessed is she who has believed, because the things promised her by the Lord shall be accomplished.* (Lk 1 45)

The next major feast of Mary takes place on the Saturday following the second Sunday after Pentecost. It is that of the Immaculate Heart of Mary. The feast is celebrated the day after the feast of the Sacred Heart of Jesus. This was an optional memorial which has recently been changed into an obligatory memorial by a Vatican decree, issued with the approval of Pope John Paul II, dated January 1, 1996. In the opening prayer for the Mass the priest says: *Father, you prepared the heart of the Virgin Mary to be a fitting home for your Holy Spirit. By her prayers may we become a more worthy temple of your glory.*

Our Lady of Mount Carmel is an optional memorial on July 16. The feast was established in 1726 to commorate the apparition of Our Lady to St Simon Stock on July 1251. The opening prayer is: *Father may the prayers of the Virgin Mary protect us and help us to reach Christ her Son . . .*

On August 5 we have the beautiful feast of the Dedication of St Mary Major. St Mary's is a basilica built in Rome to commemorate the dogma of Mary's divine Maternity declared in the Council of Ephesus in 431. In this mass part of the opening prayers says: *Lord pardon the sins of your people. May the prayers of Mary, the Mother of your Son, help to save us, for by ourselves we cannot please you.*

The great feast of the Assumption of Mary into heaven is celebrated on August 15. In the entrance prayer we sing: *All honor to you, Mary! Today you were raised above the choirs of angels to lasting glory with Christ.*

The Queenship of Mary is celebrated on August 22. This feast was instituted by Pope Pius XII in 1954. Since we consider Christ our King, it must follow that his Mother is the Queen, because she was so intimate with him in his Redemption. She is the mediatrix of all graces. This does not mean that she is the source of grace, but that she is the path or channel through which all graces come. The opening prayer for this Mass is: *Father, you have given us the Mother of your Son to be our queen and mother. With the support of her prayers may we come to share the glory of your children in the Kingdom of heaven.*

A couple of weeks later on September 8, we have the tender feast of the Birth of Mary, nine months after her Immaculate Conception. After the importance of her Son in human history Mary is next in glory. Her coming into the world caused great joy in heaven. The Mother of God, chosen from all eternity enters to begin her vocation and grow in grace. She has been given the greatest vocation ever given to a creature of God. The entrance antiphon of the Mass shouts out: *Let us celebrate with joyful hearts the birth of the Virgin Mary, of whom was born the Son of justice, Christ our Lord.*

So the first liturgical feast of our Mother begins with her Immaculate Conception and ends with her Birth, but throughout the year there are so many feasts in the countries of the world that nearly every day we could have a feast to celebrate the Blessed Virgin.

Every Saturday of the year is a day for Mary. The whole of May is her month and in October we are asked to remember in a special way the Holy Rosary, Mary's powerful prayer. October 7 is a very special feast of Our Lady of the Rosary. This feast commemorates the victory the Christian fleets had over the Turks at Lepanto in 1571. Pope St Pius V attributed this victory to the recitation of the Rosary. It prevented the Turks from overtaking Europe.

As we go through some of the great days in which Mary's life is pointed out we can see the wonders of her *Magnificat* in which she said, inspired by the Holy Spirit, *all generations shall call me blessed.* It is also wonderful to notice that the Church teaches us, in the Masses of her honor, how to ask Mary to pray for us - to be our intercessor - our mediatrix.

5

Our Lady in the Bible

All the heroic women in the old testament are in some way prefigures of the Blessed Virgin, who was in the mind of God before creation. In the eighth chapter of Proverbs we understand Our Mother saying: *The Lord possessed me in the beginning of his ways, before he made anything from the beginning. I was set up from eternity, and old before the earth was made. The depths were not as yet, and I was already conceived, neither had the fountains of water as yet sprung out: The mountains with their huge bulk had not yet been established; before the hills I was brought forth: He had not yet made the earth, nor the poles of the world.*

I was with him forming all the things; and was delighted every day, playing before him at all times; playing in the world: And my delights were to be with the children of men.

Now therefore, ye children, hear me: Blessed are they that keep my ways. Hear instruction and be wise, and refuse it not. Blessed is the man that heareth me and that watcheth daily at my gates, and waiteth at the post of my doors. He that shall find me, shall find life, and shall have salvation from the Lord: But he that shall sin against me, shall hurt his own soul. All that hate me, love death.

The Annunciation

When we eventually see Mary in the New Testament; she is praying in her home in Nazareth, a little town in Galilee, a town which had not been mentioned in the Bible before. The Angel Gabriel appears before her. St Luke records it with simplicity: *Now in the sixth month the angel Gabriel was sent from God to a town of Galilee called Nazareth to a virgin betrothed to a man named Joseph, of the house of David, and the virgin's name was Mary. And when the angel had come to her, he said, 'Hail, full of grace, the Lord is with thee. Blessed are thou among women.' When she had heard him she was troubled at his word, and kept pondering what manner of greeting this might be.*

And the angel said to her, 'Do not be afraid, Mary, for thou hast found grace with God. Behold, thou shalt conceive in thy womb and shalt bring forth a Son; and thou shalt call his name Jesus. He shall be great, and shall be called the Son of the Most High; and the Lord God will give him the throne of David his father, and he shall be king over the house of Jacob for ever; and of his kingdom there shall be no end.'

But Mary said to the angel, 'How shall this happen, since I do not know man?'

And the angel answered and said to her, 'the Holy Spirit shall come upon thee and the power of the Most High shall overshadow thee; and therefore the Holy One to be born shall be called the Son of God. And behold, Elizabeth, thy kinswoman also has conceived a son in her old age, and she who was called barren is now in her sixth month; for nothing shall be impossible with God.'

But Mary said, 'Behold the handmaid of the Lord; be it done to me according to thy word.' And the angel departed from her. (Lk 1 26-38)

I knelt on the spot where the incarnation all began, almost two thousand years ago. For me it was a dream come true - to be there in Nazareth where the Annunciation took place; to almost feel the most important event in all history; to say the Angelus with more meaning than ever before; to know even more why all the great artists of the ages have and continue to paint this scene.

It was that moment in history when Our Blessed Lady by her *fiat - thy will be done* became the Mother of God, and the world would never be the same. It was that moment when God looked down on a weary world and lovingly had his Son start his human way into all our lives. It was the beginning of a brighter world which would eventually open the gates to those who would return love for Love and forever enjoy the presence of God.

It was also the beginning of Mary's great joy and great sorrow, for she knew even then that her Son had been conceived to redeem us by his life and death. She knew this from the instruction which she received from the angel and by the interior light that she received from the Holy Spirit.

The Visitation

Mary, concerned, set out from Nazareth in Galilee to visit her cousin Elizabeth who lived close to Jerusalem, in Ain Karem. The journey took probably three days, very much the journey Our Lady would take to Bethlehem, nine months later.

In St Luke's gospel we are told: *Now in those days Mary arose and went with haste into the hill country, to a town of Juda. She entered the house of Zuchary and saluted Elizabeth. And it came to pass, when Elizabeth heard the greeting of Mary, that the babe in her womb leapt. And Elizabeth was filled with the Holy Spirit, and cried out with a loud voice, saying, 'Blessed art thou among women and blessed is the fruit of thy womb! And how have I deserved that the mother of my Lord should come to visit me? For behold, the moment the sound of thy greeting came to my ears, the babe in my womb leapt for joy. And blessed is she who has believed, because the things promised her by the Lord shall be accomplished.'*

> *And Mary said,*
> *'My soul magnifies the Lord,*
> *and my spirit rejoices in God my Savior;*
> *because he has regarded the lowliness of his handmaid;*
> *for behold, henceforth all generations shall call me blessed;*

because he who is mighty has done great things for me,
and holy is his name:
And his mercy is from generation to generation on those who fear him.
He has shown might with his arm,
he has scattered the proud in the conceit of their heart.
He has put down the mighty from their thrones and has exalted the lowly.
He has filled the hungry with good things and the rich he has sent away empty.
He has given help to Israel, his servant, mindful of his mercy -
even as he spoke to our Fathers -
to Abraham and his posterity forever.'

And Mary remained with her about three months and returned to her own house.
(Lk 1 39-56)

The Birth of Christ

The next time we hear of Mary in the Gospel of St Luke she is about to have a baby. According to the Old Testament the Child - the Savior would be born in

Bethlehem. So, *Now it came to pass in those days, that a decree went forth from Caesar Augustus that a census of the whole world should be taken. This first census took place while Cyrinus was governor of Syria. And all were going, each to his own town, to register.*

And Joseph also went from Galilee out of the town of Nazareth into Judea to the town of David, which is called Bethlehem - because he was of the house and family of David - to register, together with Mary his espoused wife, who was with child. And it came to pass while they were there, that the days for her to be delivered were fulfilled. And she brought forth her firstborn Son, and wrapped him in swaddling clothes, and laid him in a manger, because there was no room for them in the inn.

And there were shepherds in the same district living in the fields and keeping watch over their flock by night. And behold, an angel of the Lord stood by them and the glory of God shone round them, and they feared exceedingly.

And the angel said to them, 'Do not be afraid, for behold, I bring you good news of great joy which shall be to all the people, for today in the town of David a Savior has been born to you: You will find an infant wrapped in swaddling clothes and lying in a manger.' And suddenly there was with the angel a multitude of the heavenly host praising God and saying, 'Glory to God in the highest, and on earth peace among men of good will.'

And then it came to pass, when the angels had departed from them into heaven, that the shepherds were saying to one another, 'Let us go over to Bethlehem and see this thing that has come to pass, which the Lord has made known to us.'

So they went with haste, and they found Mary and Joseph, and the babe lying in the manger. And when they had seen, they understood what had been told them concerning this child. And all who heard marveled at the things told them by the shepherds. But Mary kept in mind all these things, pondering them in her heart. And the shepherds returned, glorifying and praising God for all that they had heard and seen, even as it was spoken to them. (Lk 2 1-20)

Before the shepherds came to adore the Christ child Mary looked at her baby, born in extreme poverty and she adored him, her God who had come to the world. She knew as she laid him in the warm manger, in the little town of Bethlehem (House of

Bread), that one of the principal means her Son would use for our salvation, would be to institute the Holy Eucharist, the Bread of our souls (Pere de Machault).

Adoration of the Magi

Now that Christ had been adored by the chosen people, his Mother and his foster father and the humble shepherds, he was to be adored by the gentiles. *When Jesus was born in Bethlehem of Juda, in the days of King Herod, behold, Magi came from the East to Jerusalem, saying, 'Where is he that is born King of the Jews? For we have seen his star in the East and have come to worship him.' But when King Herod heard this, he was troubled, and so was all Jerusalem with him. And gathering together all the chief priests and Scribes of the people, he inquired of them where the Christ was to be born. And they said to him, 'In Bethlehem of Judea; for thus it is written by the prophet, 'And thou, Bethlehem of the land of Juda; for from thee shall come forth a leader who shall rule my people Israel.'*

Then Herod summoned the Magi secretly, and carefully ascertained from them the time when the star had appeared to them. And sending them to Bethlehem, he said, 'Go and make careful inquiry concerning the child, and when you have found him, bring me word, that I too may go and worship him.'

Now they, having heard the King, went their way. And behold, the star that they had seen in the East went before them, until it came and stood over the place where the child was. And when they saw the star they rejoiced exceedingly. And entering the house, they found the child with Mary his Mother, and falling down they worshiped him. And opening their treasures they offered him gifts of gold, frankincense and myrrh. And being warned in a dream not to return to Herod, they went back to their own country by another way. (Mt 2 1-12)

The Presentation

It was probably before the visit of the Magi that Mary and Joseph took the Child to the Temple to be circumcised. St Luke tells us, *And when the days of her purification were fulfilled according to the Law of Moses, they took him up to Jerusalem to present him to the Lord - as it is written in the Law of the Lord, 'Every male that opens the womb shall be called holy to the Lord' - and to offer a sacrifice according to what is said in the Law of the Lord, 'a pair of turtle doves or two young pigeons.'*

And behold, there was in Jerusalem a man named Simeon, and this man was just and devout, looking for the consolation of Israel, and the Holy Spirit was upon him. And it had been revealed to him by the Holy Spirit that he should not see death before he had seen the Christ of the Lord. And he came by inspiration of the Spirit into the Temple. And when his parents brought in the Child Jesus, to do for him according to the custom of the Law, he also received him into his arms and blessed God, saying, 'Now thou dost dismiss thy servant, O Lord, according to thy word, in peace; because my eyes have seen thy salvation, which thou hast prepared before the face of all peoples: a light of revelation to the Gentiles and a glory for thy people Israel.'

And his father and mother were marveling at the things spoken concerning him. And Simeon blessed them, and said to Mary his mother, 'Behold, this child is destined for the fall and for the rise of many in Israel, and for a sign that shall be contradicted. And thy own soul a sword shall pierce, that the thoughts of many hearts may be revealed.'
(Lk 2 22-35)

Mary experienced the first of the seven sorrows that the Church lists as overwhelming pains that pierced the Immaculate and Sorrowful Heart of Mary. While from the very conception Our Lady knew that her Son was born to suffer and die for our sins, she accepted joyfully all pain she was to feel.

Flight into Egypt

The second great sorrow that Mary was to experience shortly after this, was having to pack up in a hurry and take Jesus into Egypt to save him from the madness of Herod. St Matthew tells us that as soon as the Magi departed, *behold, an angel of the Lord appeared in a dream to Joseph, saying, 'Arise, and take the child and his mother, and flee into Egypt, and remain there until I tell thee. For Herod will seek the child to destroy him.' So he arose, and took the child and his mother by night, and withdrew into Egypt, and remained there until the death of Herod.* (Mt 2 13-15)

Herod had all the two years old and under boys of Bethlehem and its neighborhood killed. They were the first martyrs to give their lives for Christ, and were given Baptism with their blood. So we might say that the millions of babies who are aborted every year in our modern times are our new martyrs, killed by the madness of modern people. The sorrow of Mary was increased with the knowledge that the power of her age, in her land, wanted to kill the Son of God, who had come to save the world.

Jesus Lost in the Temple

Eventually Jesus returned to Israel with Mary and Joseph and went to live in Nazareth, where Joseph worked as a carpenter, close to the house where Jesus had been conceived. I have been fortunate to visit the place which is considered to be the house where Jesus grew up and worked also as a carpenter, before he entered his public life. It was here that *he grew and became strong. He was full of wisdom and the grace of God was upon him.* And it was from here, when he was twelve years old that he went with Mary and Joseph to Jerusalem to celebrate the Feast of the Passover. *And after they had fulfilled the days, when they were returning, the boy Jesus remained in Jerusalem, and his parents did not know it. But thinking that he was in the caravan, they had come a day's journey before it occurred to them to look for him among their relatives and acquaintances. And not finding him they returned to Jerusalem in search of him.*

And it came to pass after three days, that they found him in the temple, sitting in the midst of the teachers, listening to them and asking them questions. And all who were listening to him were amazed at his understanding and his answers. And when they saw him they were astonished. And his mother said to him, 'Son, why hast thou done so to us? Behold, in sorrow thy father and I have been seeking thee.'

And he said to them, 'How is it that you sought me? Did you not know that I must be about my Father's business?' And they did not understand the word that he spoke to them.

And he went down with them; and came to Nazareth, and was subject to them; and his mother kept all these things carefully in her heart. And Jesus advanced in wisdom and age and grace before God and man. (Lk 2 43-52)

Losing her Son for three days was the third sword that pierced Our Lady's heart. She must have known that the time for his public life had not yet come. Just as she feared for his life when he was a baby, she must have feared when she found that he was not with the group returning to Nazareth.

The Marriage Feast at Cana

It must have been soon after Christ began his public life of teaching in and about Galilee that he and his Mother were invited to a wedding at Cana, a little town close to Nazareth. St John tells us that the disciples of Jesus were also invited. *And the wine having run short, the mother of Jesus said to him, 'they have no wine.' And Jesus said to her, 'What wouldst thou have me do, woman? My hour has not yet come.' His mother said to the attendant, "Do whatever he tells you.'*

Now six stone water jars were placed there, after the Jewish manner of purification, each holding two or three measures. Jesus said to them, 'Fill the jars with water.' And they filled them to the brim. And Jesus said to them, 'Draw out now, and take to the chief steward.' And they took it to him.

Now when the chief steward had tasted the water after it had become wine, not knowing whence it was (though the attendants who had drawn the water knew), the chief steward called the bridegroom, and said to him, 'Every man at first sets forth the good wine, and when they have drunk freely, then that which is poorer. But thou hast kept the good wine until now.'

This first of his signs Jesus worked at Cana of Galilee; and he manifested his glory, and his disciples believed in him. (Jn 2 3-11)

Our Lady spoke the last words we hear from her in the Gospel. She said, *'Do whatever he tells you.'* The first words we hear from her at the Annunciation are, *'Your will be done.'* None knew or still know Jesus as his Mother did and does. She was sure that he would help the bridegroom and perform his first miracle at the request of his Mother. He still does. Her intercession is now more apparent than ever.

Jesus and His Brethren

Our Lord must have been well into his public life when St Matthew relates the following happening. By this time Christ had performed many of his miracles. *While he (Jesus) was still speaking to the crowd, his mother and his brethren were standing outside, seeking to speak to him. And someone said to him, 'Behold, thy mother and thy brethren are standing outside, seeking thee.' But he answered and said to him who told him, 'Who is my mother and who are my brethren?' And stretching forth his hand towards his disciples, he said, 'Behold my mother and my brethren! For whoever does the will of my Father in heaven, he is my brother and sister and mother.'* (Mt 12 46-50)

In no way is Jesus making little of his Mother. He knows that there never was or ever will be anyone who does the will of his Father as his Mother. At that moment he knew that from the moment of her conception she was free from sin; that her whole life was sinless. He also knew that none like her would share in his passion and death.

He is giving a lesson to those who listened then and for everyone between them and the end of the world. The lesson is, we all are created to do the Will of God and in doing so, in this world and in the next we will be happy.

Mary at the Cross

We do not know for certain where Our Lady was on the first Holy Thursday when her Son instituted the Holy Eucharist, at the Last Supper - his last celebration of the Passover in the upper room in Jerusalem. Where was she as he suffered his agony in the Garden of Gethsemane? Where was she as he was apprehended and taken to be tried as a criminal? Perhaps she was with the other holy women. But we do know that she was in Jerusalem on the following day when Jesus would be condemned to death and forced to take a cross upon his shoulders and walk through the streets of the city to Calvary.

She was there. We meet her at the fourth station - very close to where he was given the cross. She must have picked that spot to meet him. And when their eyes met sorrow filled the world so much that it overflowed, but the love was so strong between Son and Mother - God and his most perfect creature - that the world was to change forever.

Mary walked while her Son and God shuffled, because he was so weak from mistreatment of his captors, he was unable to raise his feet to walk. Every moment of Christ's suffering as he made his way to Calvary pierced Mary's Immaculate Heart. It was the fourth sword.

Eventually the sad and weary group - Christ being helped by Simon, Mary with St John and the other two Marys, Mary of Cleophas and Mary Magdalene, some soldiers and some official jews - arrived at the place of the skull. Joseph of Arimathea and Nicodemus must also have been there, because they helped to take Christ's body from the cross after one of the soldiers, making sure that Christ was dead, opened his side with a lance.

Mary could not take her eyes from her dying Son as he hung on the crude cross. And the fifth sword pierced her heart, and when the lance was plunged into the dead Christ the sixth sword went through the suffering heart of his Mother.

St John tells us: *Now there were standing by the cross of Jesus his mother and his mother's sister, Mary of Cleophas, and Mary Magdalene. When Jesus, therefore, saw his mother and the disciple standing by, whom he loved, he said to his mother, 'Woman, behold, thy son!' Then he said to the disciple, 'Behold thy mother.' And from that hour the disciple took her into his home.* (Jn 19 25-27)

Pope Paul II in his Apostolic Letter, *Salcifici Doloris*, writes: *It was on Calvary that Mary's suffering, besides the suffering of Jesus, reached an intensity which can hardly be imagined from a human point of view, but which was mysteriously and supernaturally faithful for the Redemption of the world. Her ascent of Calvary and her standing at the foot of the cross, together with the beloved disciple were a special sort of sharing in the redeeming death of her Son.*

Christ's body was taken from the cross and was readied for burial. It was then that the seventh sword entered the Suffering and Immaculate Heart of Mary. Is it no wonder that her beloved Son wants her honored under that title.

6

Apparitions of Our Lady

Since Our Blessed Lady was assumed into heaven almost two thousand years ago, she has paid many visits to our world, even up to modern times. To list and give a little account of only some of these visit would take the writing of many books.

I shall highlight only four of the many apparitions which have taken place throughout the years. For a fuller account, one might read Don Sharkey's wonderful book *The Woman Shall Conquer,* published by the Franciscans of Marytown in 1973.

The visits of Our Lady always reflect the state of the world at the time she appears. There is always a reason which has been mainly a loving warning to repentance and penance, to prayer.

The four visits I relate are spread out from 1531 to 1917 - about four hundred years. I have been fortunate to visit all four places. There have always been thousands visiting Guadalupe, many walking many miles and falling on their knees at a great distance from the miraculous picture. From there they approach Our Lady on their knees. Each time I visited Lourdes, there were thousands visiting the grotto, seeking help from Our Mother. I have been privileged to meet the parents of Francisco and Jacinta and the sister of Lucia at Fatima years ago when the place was much quieter than it is today. It seemed to be so remote then. The afternoon I got to Fatima in the Summer of 1953, there was a total of about 16 pilgrims. I know Knock so well, because for more than twenty years, I have been making an annual pilgrimage - keeping up a tradition began over one hundred years ago when the first pilgrimage was made by a group of men from Limerick. I always like to think that perhaps my grandfather was one of those men.

The reason for our visits to these holy spots is to ask Mary to bring us closer to her Son, which is the greatest desire she has.

Our Lady of Guadalupe -1531

During the ten-year period between the conquest of Mexico and Our Lady's apparition, very few Indians (Aztecs) were converted. But seven years after the apparition, over five million Aztecs converted to the Catholic faith. This is indeed a greater miracle than the wonderful image Our Lady left, since there were so few priests and they had very little knowledge of the Nahuatl tongue.

On the morning of Saturday, December 9, 1531, a poor Indian, named Juan Diego, recently converted to the Faith, was on his way to Mass at one of the mission churches in Mexico City, when he first encountered a beautiful lady. She told him that she was the ever Virgin, Holy Mary, Mother of the true God and that she wished that a church be erected to her in the place where she stood. She asked that he should go to the Bishop and tell him of her request.

The Bishop was more than perplexed at the request and dismissed him saying that he would think about it. Juan Diego was wise enough to know that Our Lady's request had fallen on deaf ears, so he returned that evening to where he had seen Our Lady. She was waiting for him. He suggested that she should send someone to whom the Bishop would listen. Our

Lady told him that he was the one chosen, so he had to go back again and tell the Bishop that it was the Virgin Mary, Mother of the true God, who sent him.

He did return to the Bishop the following day and was told that he had to bring a sign before the Bishop would act. He again saw Our Lady who promised him the sign.

On December 12, Juan Diego set out early to find a priest for his dying uncle. He did not want to see Our Lady, whom he thought would detain him, so he took another route, but she was there. He explained to her that he had been unable to visit her the day before because his uncle was sick and now he was on his way to find a priest.

Our Lady told him that he should not worry about his uncle; that he was already cured. She told Juan Diego to climb the hill to the place he had first seen her, and to pick as many roses as he was able to carry. He brought down an armful of beautiful fresh roses, even though it was the middle of winter and not the season for roses. Our Lady arranged them in Juan Diego's tilma, telling him that this was the sign which he should take to the Bishop.

He was eventually brought before the Bishop, where he unfolded his tilma to let the roses fall at the

Bishop's feet. They did. However, the eyes of the Bishop were not directed towards the roses, but were fixed on the tilma, where he saw imprinted the image of Our Lady of Guadalupe, as Juan Diego had described her.

It was Our Lady who had given to Juan Diego, the name Guadalupe, which means *the one who crushed the serpent.* Over two hundred years later when Pope Benedict heard the story of Our Lady of Guadalupe and saw her picture he fell on his knees and said: *He has not done in like manner to every nation.*

Our Lady of Guadalupe is not just for Mexico; She is for all the Americas. In 1945, Pope Pius XII sent a radio message to Mexico and all America, placing the whole Western Hemisphere under her care. He said . . . *May you keep forever under your powerful patronage the purity and integrity of our Holy Mother, both in Mexico and in the entire American continent. For we know that as long as you all acknowledge her as Queen and Mother, America and Mexico are safe.*

Lourdes - 1858

In 1830, Our Lady came to visit St Catherine Laboure, in Paris. She gave her the miraculous medal. Again in 1836, Our Lady comes to Paris to speak to Fr Charles du Friche des Gennettes while he was saying Mass at the Church of Our Lady of Victories. Father was discouraged that so few came to Mass. In his distress, he heard a voice say: *Consecrate your parish to the Most Holy and Immaculate Heart of Mary*. He did and Mass attendance grew to greater numbers. In 1846, Our Lady comes again to France to the little village of LaSalette in the southeast, where she weeps for the sins of the world.

In 1854 on December 8, Pope Pius IX declared the doctrine *which states that the Blessed Virgin Mary was preserved and exempted from all stain of original sin from the first instant of her conception in view of the merits of Jesus Christ, the Savior of all mankind, is a doctrine revealed by God and which, for this reason, all Christians are bound to believe firmly and with confidence . . . .* In a world which seemed to have put to death the Catholic Faith, the Holy Father boldly proclaimed the doctrine of the Immaculate Conception of the Blessed Virgin.

It was a cold day on February 11, 1858, when Bernadette Soubirous, age fourteen, her sister and her friend went out from the little village of Lourdes in the south of France, close to the Spanish border, to gather fire wood. Bernadette being in poor health was slower than the others who ran off leaving her to trail them. Stopping to take off her shoes before crossing a stream, she heard a noise like a hard wind. Looking straight ahead she saw a beautiful lady, high above the grotto standing on a ledge, across the stream.

The amazed Bernadette was beckoned by the smiling lady to move closer. All fear left her; she took out her rosary, falling on her knees, she began to pray. As Bernadette began to say the Rosary, she noticed that the Lady's fingers went from bead to bead on her own rosary, joining in only on the recital of the *Glory be to the Father.* When the Rosary was finished, the Lady went from the ledge to the interior of the rocky grotto.

Bernadette saw the lady nineteen times in all. She and all the local people were convinced that it was the Blessed Virgin. However, it was not until towards the end of the visits that Bernadette asked the lady who she was. After the third request as Bernadette later recorded: *the lady was standing above the rose bush, in a position being like that seen on the miraculous medal. Her face became more serious and she seemed to bow in a humble way. She then joined her hands, raising them to her breast. She looked upwards to heaven, slowly opened her hands and leaning towards me, said in a voice full of emotion: I am the Immaculate Conception.*

During the many visits Our Lady had requested pray and penance; she promised to make Bernadette happy in the next world, but not in this one. She revealed a spring, the water, which was to be the instrument of many miraculous cures.

After much harassment from the local authorities things settled down. The grotto which had been fenced in was opened up and people began to flock there from all over France and many experienced cures of soul and body.

Bernadette became a nun and found little happiness as Our Lady predicted. The spring was not for her; she died in 1879 at the age of thirty-five. She was canonized on the Feast of the Immaculate Conception in 1933 by Pope Pius XI.

Knock - 1879

It was raining softly on the evening of August 21, 1879, when, in the small village of Knock, Mayo, the most western county of Ireland, fourteen people, ages from six to seventy-five, saw the Blessed Virgin Mary and with her St Joseph and St John the Evangelist. Our Lady, dressed in white, was wearing a gold crown, the center figure, was taller and stood out in front of the others. St Joseph was on her right and St John on the left.

The apparition bathed in a mysterious light, lasted for about two hours at the south gable of the church. To the left of St John there was a simple altar on which stood a young lamb; behind him was a large cross. The lamb was surrounded by angels, whose wings were fluttering, but whose faces were unseen, since they were turned away from those who looked at the scene.

A fifteenth witness, Patrick Walsh, saw the strange light from about half mile away. When he asked about it the following day, he was told about the apparition.

While the rain continued the figures and the place where they appeared remained dry. Patrick Hill who was fourteen, said that the figures were *full round* and the book which St John held contained *lines and letters*. One of the women present moved towards Our Lady to embrace her feet but found nothing in her arms. Our Lady receded from her.

Our Lady came to Knock to console a weary nation; to encourage the people by her presence; and to tell them by her silence that they were not forgotten by her Son; the Second Person of the Holy Trinity. Ever since St Patrick held up the three-leaved shamrock to explain the great mystery, the Holy Trinity was forever in the hearts of the Irish.

The 1800s had been a wicked time for Ireland. The 1845-46 famine had taken over a million people by cruel death and sent another million into exile. The west of Ireland, for all its great beauty, was the hardest hit. And now in the never-to-be-forgotten year of 1879 there was still another potato blight which was the worst to show itself in Mayo since 1847.

Mary McLaughlin, the priest's housekeeper, who was among those witnessing the apparition, went to tell Archdeacon Cavanagh about what was happening. He misunderstood her, thinking that the event had passed and he did not go to the scene. He always regretted that he had not seen the most wonderful happening that had ever been witnessed in the west of Ireland.

Within a few weeks the Archbishop of Tuam, the Most Reverend John MacHale, appointed a three-priest commission to investigate the apparition; which reported that the testimony of all was trustworthy and satisfactory. However, the Archbishop decided not to make a pronouncement. In 1936, Archbishop Gilmartin appointed another commission. The two surviving witnesses as well as many who claimed to have been cured at Knock gave evidence and the report was sent to Rome. There were cures very soon after the apparition which Archdeacon Cavanagh recorded. After thousands of cures throughout the years in 1936 a scientific investigation in the form of a medical bureau was set up.

The visit of Our Lady to Knock has much significance. It occurred within the octave of the feast of the Assumption which in 1950 was declared a dogma of the Church by Pope Pius XII. Just as our Lady at Lourdes, twenty-one years before, confirmed the dogma of the Immaculate Conception. It is also of no small significance that the saints who appeared with the Blessed Virgin were St Joseph who had been the guardian of Our Lady before and after Christ's birth and St John who was her guardian after Christ's death. St Joseph, patron of the Church, looks at Our Lady in reverence and bows to her as Mother of the Church; St John holding the Mass book, stands next to the altar on which stood the sacrificial lamb, pointing out the importance of the Holy Mass, which has always been appreciated by the Irish as the center of their interior life and the soul of the Catholic Church.

Pilgrims in the hundred of thousands began to flock to Knock each year. For the hundredth anniversary of the apparition on August 21, 1979, the Holy Father, Pope John Paul II said a Mass of thanksgiving for a half million who came from all over Ireland.

It is the custom of the pilgrims to walk around the church, the gable of which was the scene of the apparition, and say the Rosary. There is a regular schedule of daily masses said at the basilica which was built for the centenary. There are masses said at the spot of the apparition which is now a beautiful chapel.

Our Lady of Knock, Queen of Ireland, you gave hope to your people in a time of distress, and comforted them in sorrow. You have inspired countless pilgrims to pray with confidence to your divine Son, remembering his promise - ask and you shall receive, seek and you shall find.

Help me to remember that we are all pilgrims on the road to heaven. Fill me with love and concern for my brothers and sisters in Christ, especially those who live with me. Comfort me when I am sick, or lonely or depressed. Teach me how to take part ever more reverently in the Holy Mass. Pray for me now, and at the hour of my death. Amen.

Fatima - 1917

It was in the Spring of 1916, when Europe in the middle of madness, the war that was suppose to end all wars, in a remote spot in Portugal called Fatima, three children, Lucia des Santos aged nine and her cousins Francisco and Jacinta Marto ages eight and seven were tending their small flock of sheep when it began to rain and the cold breeze reminded them that it was not yet summer.

Herding the sheep to the shelter of some trees, they found refuge for themselves in a shallow spot under a rock mound. Soon the sun began to shine again, but as suddenly as the rain had started, a strong wind began to blow and they saw a brightness moving from east to west in their direction. It stopped over the flat rocks which had been their protection.

Suddenly they noticed that they were in the presence of a young man *more brilliant than a crystal penetrated by the rays of the sun* as Lucia described him later.

Don't be afraid, he said. *I am the Angel of Peace. Pray with me.* He taught them a prayer.

> *My God, I believe, I adore, I hope,
> and I love you. I beg pardon of
> you for those who do not believe,
> do not adore, do not hope, and do
> not love you.*

Then he told them to use this prayer because the Hearts of Jesus and Mary would listen to them. The angel disappeared while the children continued to repeat the prayer over and over.

The angel appeared again that summer, when he told the children that they must pray a lot because the Hearts of Jesus and Mary had plans for them. He also asked them to make sacrifices as acts of reparation for sinners, telling them that he was the Guardian Angel of Portugal.

In the Fall he again appeared and once again taught them another prayer.

> *Most Holy Trinity, Father, Son, and Holy Spirit, I adore you profoundly, and I offer you the Most Precious Body, Blood, Soul and Divinity of Jesus Christ, present in all the tabernacles of the world, in reparation for the outrages, sacrileges and indifferences with which he himself is offended. And through the infinite merits of his Most Sacred Heart and of the Immaculate Heart of Mary, I beg of you the conversion of poor sinners.*

The year 1917 came and the war had become even more violent. On May 13 as they were watching their sheep at Cova da Iria they observed a flash of light so bright that they thought that it was lightning. Running from under a tree they came to a sudden halt when they saw a beautiful lady in the center of a ball of light standing on a three-foot light evergreen called azinheira.

Don't be afraid, the lady said in a reassuring voice; which put the children at ease. Lucia, without fear and with a feeling of great peace and joy asked, *Where are you from your Excellency?*

I am from heaven.

What do you want me to do?

The lady told them that she would like them to meet her five more times, once every month on the 13th day at the same place at the same time, and on the 6th visit, on October 13 that she would tell them who she was and what she wanted of them.

Francisco could see the lady, but was unable to hear what she was saying. Neither did he hear her on all the following appearances. Jacinta could both see and hear the lady, but never talked to her. It was only Lucia who carried on all the conversation with the lady during the six apparitions.

It was during the first apparition that purgatory and heaven were discussed and it became apparent to the children that the beautiful lady was the Blessed Virgin Mary, the Mother of God. Prayers and penance were requested. Our Lady asked the children to pray the Rosary every day to obtain peace for the world and the end of the war.

On June 13 Our Lady appeared again and once more asked the children to pray the Rosary. She also said that she would soon take Jacinta and Francisco but that Lucia would remain to make known the devotion to the Immaculate Heart of Mary. She promised salvation to all who embraced that devotion saying *their souls will be loved by God as flowers placed by myself to adorn his throne.*

It was during this visit that Our Lady asked the children to insert the following prayers between the mysteries when they would say the Rosary:

> *O my Jesus, forgive us our sins, save us from the fires of hell. Draw all souls to heaven, especially those in most need of your mercy.*

In anticipation of the third visit, July 13, almost five thousand people turned up at the Cova da Iria. When Our Lady appeared, Lucia again asked her who she was and requested that she perform a miracle. She was told that on October 13 the information would be given to her and a miracle would be seen.

During this visit the children were given a glimpse of hell, *where,* Our Lady said *the souls of poor sinners go. To save sinners, Our Lord wishes to establish throughout the world devotion to the Immaculate Heart. If people do what I request, many souls will be saved and there will be peace in the world.*

During this apparition also Our Lady foretold the second world war, while the first war had not yet finished.

On August 12, the children were taken to Ourem by the civil authorities for questioning, so they were unable to go to the Cova on the 13th. However, while they were tending their sheep on the 18th Our Lady appeared. Again she admonished them to pray the Rosary and to make sacrifices for sinners. *Many souls go to hell because they have no one to sacrifice or pray for them.*

On September 13, the large crowd who came to be present at the 5th apparition witnessed a glowing globe coming from the sky and hovering for awhile where Our Lady was to appear. It then vanished. Our Lady revealed herself to the three children. *Continue to pray the Rosary,* she said, *to bring about the end of the war. In October Our Lord will come, together with Our Lady of Sorrows, Our Lady of Carmel and St Joseph with the Child Jesus to bless the world.*

On the night of October 12, a hard winter wind swept from the north carrying with it a bitter rain, while thousands of pilgrims were making their way by foot and by burro to witness the miracle of Fatima promised by Our Lady. Soaked to the skin with the cold, penetrating rain their discomfort was submerged by their faith. They carried the sick and the old for miles reaching the Cova in the dark, cold, wet morning. All classes came with great expectations.

It was still raining when the children arrived to meet the Lady. Making their way through the crowd, Lucia requested that people should put down their umbrellas. One after another they obeyed without question, even though it was still raining. When Our Lady appeared those who were close noticed how Lucia's face lit up and became transparently beautiful.

At this visit Our Lady requested that a chapel be built in her honor. She told the children that she was the Lady of the Rosary and that they should continue to pray the Rosary every day. She said, *Let them offend Our Lord no more, for he is already much offended.* Then she disappeared in light and suddenly there appeared in the sky three tableaus: one of the Holy Family, Our Lady in a white dress with a blue mantle, St Joseph beside her holding the Child Jesus. The second was Our Lady of Sorrows and beside her stood her Son looking sad as when he had met her on the way to the crucifixion. He made the Sign of the cross over the crowd. The third was Our Lady of Mount Carmel, crowned as queen of the universe, with the Infant Jesus on her knee.

The crowd saw nothing of all this. What they saw afterwards was the bright sun which they could look at straight, without blinking. This scene lasted a few seconds and then the sun began to dance - to rotate rapidly like a fire-wheel. It stopped for a moment, beginning to whirl again with a greater speed. On its edge appeared a fiery red rim which flung itself across the sky, reflecting the different colors of the rainbow on the trees and earth below. Then the sun seemed to plunge toward the frightened crowd, which hugged the ground, expecting death. As suddenly as the sun had plunged towards the earth, it began to recede slowly. The whole wonder of the sun had taken place for about ten minutes. Then the crowd noticed that their clothing which had been soaked had suddenly become bone dry; they expressed great joy in laughter and tears. The miracle of Fatima had happened.

Francisco and Jacinta died in 1918, while Lucia became a nun and continues to spread devotion to the Immaculate Heart of Mary. Before she died Jacinta told Lucia to tell everyone that Our Lord grants all graces through the Immaculate Heart of Mary; that all must make their petitions through her; that the Sacred Heart of Jesus desires that the Immaculate Heart of Mary be venerated at the same time.

7

Marian Hymns

I have included just a few of the multitude of hymns that have been written to honor Our Lady. They may be used as prayers in one's private conversation with Mary and her Son.

Immaculate Mary

Immaculate Mary, your praises we sing.
You reign now in splendor with Jesus our King.

Refrain: *Ave, Ave, Ave Maria!*
            Ave, Ave, Ave Maria!

In heaven the blessed your glory proclaim.
On earth we your children invoke your sweet name.

Refrain

We pray for the Church, our true Mother on earth.
And beg you to watch o'er the land of our birth.

Refrain

Hail, Holy Queen, Enthroned Above

Hail, holy Queen, enthroned above, O Maria!
Hail, Mother of mercy and of love, O Maria!

Refrain: Triumph, all ye cherubim,
*   Sing with us, ye seraphim,*
*   Heav'n and earth resound the hymn:*
*   Salve, Salve, Salve Regina!*

O Gate of Life, we honor thee, O Maria!
Our joy, our hope, and heaven's key, O Maria!

Refrain

O Mary, hasten with thine aid, O Maria!
Most gentle, loving, joyous Maid, O Maria!

Refrain

Sing of Mary

Sing of Mary, pure and lowly,
  Virgin Mother undefiled;
Sing of God's own Son most holy,
  Who became her little child.
Fairest child of fairest mother,
  The Lord, who came to earth.
Word-made-flesh, our very brother,
  Takes our nature by his birth.

Sing of Jesus, Son of Mary,
  In the home at Nazareth.
Toil and labor cannot weary
  Love enduring unto death.
Constant was the love he gave her,
  though he went forth from her side,
Forth to preach and heal and suffer,
  'till on Calvary he died.

Lady of Knock (My Queen of Peace)

There were people of all ages,
Gathered round the gable wall.

*Poor and humble men and women
And the children that you call.
We are gathered here before you
And our hearts are just the same,
Filled with joy at such a vision
As we praise your name.*

*Golden Rose, Queen of Ireland.
All my cares and troubles see,
As I kneel with love before you
Lady of Knock, my Queen of Peace.*

*Though your message is unspoken,
Still the truth we find inside.
And I gaze upon your vision
And the truth I try to find,
Here I stand with John the Teacher
And Saint Joseph at your side.
And I see the Lamb of God
On the altar glorified.*

*And the Lamb will conquer,
And the woman clothed in the sun
Will shine her light on everyone.
And the Lamb will conquer,*

And the Woman clothed in the sun
Will shine her light on everyone.

Golden Rose, Queen of Ireland.
All my cares and troubles see,
As I kneel with love before you,
Lady of Knock, my Queen of Peace.
Lady of Knock, my Queen of Peace.

Hail, Queen of Heaven

Hail, Queen of heav'n, the Ocean Star,
Guide of the wand'rer here below!
Thrown on life's surge we claim thy care.
Save us from peril and from woe.

Mother of Christ, Star of the sea
Pray for the wand'rer, pray for me!

O gentle, chaste and spotless Maid,
We sinners make our pray'rs thro' thee;
Remind thy son that he has paid
The price of our iniquity.

Virgin most pure, Star of the sea,
Pray for the sinner, pray for me.

Sojourners in this vale of tears,
To thee blest advocate we cry.
O pity our sorrows, calm our fears,
And soothe with hope our misery.

Refuge in grief, Star of the sea,
Pray for the mourner, pray for me!

And while to him, who reigns above,
In Godhead, one in persons three,
The source of life, of grace, of love,
Homage we pay on bended knee.

Do thou, bright Queen, Star of the sea
Pray for thy children, pray for me!

On This Day, O Beautiful Mother

Refrain:
On this day O beautiful Mother,
On this day we give you our love.

Near you, Madonna keep us forever,
Trusting in your constant love.

On this day we ask to share,
Dearest Mother your good care:
Aid us lest our heart one day,
Wander from your guiding way.

Refrain

Queen of Angels, deign to hear,
Men and women in their prayer;
Young hearts too, O Virgin pure,
Their salvation do assure.

Refrain

O Most Holy One

O most holy one, O most lowly one,
Dearest Virgin Maria!
Mother of fair love, home of the Spirit Dove,
Ora, ora pro nobis.

Help in sadness drear, port of gladness near,
Virgin Mother Maria!
In pity heeding, hear our pleading,
Ora, ora pro nobis.

Mother, maiden fair, look with loving care,
Hear our prayer, O Maria!
Our sorrow feeling, send us thy healing,
Ora, ora pro nobis.

Daily, Daily Sing to Mary

Daily, daily sing to Mary;
Sing, my soul, her praises due;
All her feasts, her actions honor,
With the heart's devotion true.
Lost in wond'ring contemplation,
Be her majesty confest;
Call her Mother, call her Virgin,
Happy Mother, Virgin blest.

She is mighty in her pleading,
Tender in her loving care;
Ever watchful, understanding,

All our sorrows she will share.
Advocate and loving Mother,
Mediatrix of all grace!
Heaven's blessings she dispenses,
On our sinful human race.

Sing my tongue, the Virgin's trophies,
Who for us, her Maker bore;
For the curse of old inflicted,
Peace and blessing to restore.
Sing in songs of praise unending,
Sing the world's majestic Queen;
Weary not, nor faint in telling
All the gifts she gives to men.

All my senses, heart, affections,
Strive to sound her glory forth.
Spread abroad the sweet memorials
Of the Virgin's priceless worth.
Where the voice of music thrilling,
Where the tongues of eloquence,
That can utter befitting all
Her matchless excellence?

Mother of Christ

Mother of Christ, Mother of Christ,
What shall I ask of Thee?
I do not sigh for the wealth of the earth,
For the joys that fade and flee,
But,
Mother of Christ, Mother of Christ,
This do I long to see,
The bliss untold which thine arms enfold,
The treasure upon Thy knee.

Mother of Christ, Mother of Christ,
What shall I do for Thee?
I will love Thy son with the whole of my strength,
My only King shall he be.
Yes,
Mother of Christ, Mother of Christ,
This will I do for Thee,
Of all that are dear or cherished here,
None shall be dear as he.

Mother of Christ, Mother of Christ,
I toss on a stormy sea,
O lift Thy child as a beacon light

To the port where I fain would be.
And,
Mother of Christ, Mother of Christ,
This do I ask of Thee;
When the voyage is o'er, O stand on the shore and
Show him at last to me.

8

Special Devotions

Holy Rosary

When we speak of devotions to Mary we usually bring to mind the Holy Rosary, which is a panorama of the lives of Jesus and Mary, starting with the Annunciation -- the conception of Christ and ending with the Coronation of the Blessed Virgin. It has been recommended by saints and popes throughout the ages.

Among the different ways of praying, there is none more excellent than the Rosary. It condenses into itself all the devotion that is due to Mary. It is the remedy for all our evils, the root of all our blessings. (Pope Leo XIII)

St Pope Pius X who had a great love for Mary says: *Of all prayers the Rosary is the most beautiful and the richest in graces; of all it is the one which is most pleasing to Mary, the Virgin most Holy.*

Therefore, love the Rosary and recite it every day with devotion. This is the testament which I leave to you, so that you may remember me by it.

We all know that the greatest form of worship is the Holy Mass. We can find Mary there, too. When the bread and wine is changed by the priest into the body, blood, soul and divinity of Christ, we must realize that it was Mary who gave him his body and blood, and when Christ's sacrifice is once again offered to his Father, as it is in every Mass, Mary is there as she was at the foot of the cross.

The Angelus and Regina Caeli

The Angelus is said at noon every day to remind us of the greatest moment in the whole of time, the moment when Christ was conceived when Mary said *yes*. It may also be said at 6 p.m. During Easter time, the Regina Caeli is said in place of the Angelus. This prayer is also addressed to Mary, reminding us that it was she who gave birth to Christ who on the third day after his awful death arose gloriously from the dead. We rejoice in his conception; we rejoice in his resurrection.

The Month of May

Perhaps it is the most beautiful month. Life which seems to have died during the winter, shows itself again in Spring and by the time May arrives we see nature in all its glory — fresh and beautiful. We see the beauty of God's work. In Our Lady we see the most beautiful creation from God's hand. It is most suitable that we give the month of May to Mary. It is a time for special devotion, processions, visits to her shrines and a time to encourage our children. *O Mary, we crown thee with blossoms today; Queen of the Angels, Queen of the May.* A year in which we give May to Our Lady will be a year where we will get closer to her Son.

The month of October is one devoted to the Holy Rosary - another month to put Mary's devotion on the top of our list!

Novenas to Mary

Dotted throughout the Liturgical year, we find beautiful feasts of Our Lady. To get the maximum from those wonderful days, we can stretch them by starting the celebration nine days before the feast. It is a custom, beloved by the Church and very fruitful to our spiritual life. While we may make novenas for every feast of Our Lady, the popular ones are before the Immaculate Conception, the Nativity of Our Lady, the Annunciation, the Seven Sorrows of Our Lady and the Assumption. In Ireland, August 13 is a special day - the day that begins the novena to Our Lady of Knock for the feast which is celebrated on August 21.

The Brown Scapular

A very fine devotion to Our Lady is the wearing of the Scapular of Our Lady of Mount Carmel - a custom of long standing in the Church.

The Order of Mount Carmel was founded in the twelfth century by a Calabrian priest, and claims to carry on the centuries-old monastic tradition of Mount Carmel which is supposed to go back to the prophet Elias.

On July 16, 1251, Our Lady appeared to St Simon Stock, the Superior General of the Order, and promised special blessings to all its members and all who wore its habit. Since then, the Church has solemnly and repeatedly furthered this devotion (the wearing of the scapular) which began in England. For centuries Catholics have taken advantage of the protection promised by Our Lady. The devout use of the scapular shows our trust in the Blessed Virgin's motherly aid to help us at the hour of our death.

The feast of Our Lady of Mount Carmel was instituted for the Carmelites in 1332, and extended to the whole Church by Pope Benedict XIII in 1726.

The Sorrowful and Immaculate Heart of Mary

The feast of the Sorrowful and Immaculate Heart of Mary is celebrated on the Saturday after the feast of the Sacred Heart of Jesus. It is well placed because this devotion ties in very much with the devotion to the Sacred Heart of Jesus. It was Pope Pius XII who instituted the feast for the whole Church. While it is certainly not a new devotion, it's one for our times. St John Eudes (1601-1680) tied this devotion to that of the Sacred Heart of Jesus. The devotion began to gain popularity at the beginning of the nineteenth century in France, helped by the introduction of the Miraculous Medal given to St Catherine Laboure in 1830. Then on December 8, 1854, Pope Pius IX declared the dogma of the Immaculate Conception. The visits of Our Lady at Fatima in 1917 sealed this devotion. In 1956, Pope Pius XII urged that the faithful should unite the devotion to the Sacred Heart of Jesus to that of the

Immaculate Heart of Mary (*Haurietis Aquas* #124). He had already consecrated the world in 1942, when the war was creating havoc, to the Immaculate Heart of Mary.

The first Saturday of every month is especially set aside for this devotion as is the first Friday of every month a special day for devotion to the Sacred Heart of Jesus.

Special Prayers

The Memorare is a wonderful prayer invoking the aid of Mary. Next to the Hail Mary, it flies like an arrow to tell Our Lady of our needs. The Litany of Loretto is said many times after the Holy Rosary. Mary is invoked under so many titles. Each country has Mary as their special patron under a special title. The USA has two - the Immaculate Conception and Our Lady of Guadalupe.

9

Aspirations

Our ambition, here on earth, should be to be continually in the presence of God. While our days are full of work, fulfilling our vocation, we may still be in the presence of God and in turn, make our work an act of prayer. The saying of aspirations from time to time keeps our mind on God. I am listing a few addressed to Our Lady. The reader may make up his or her own.

O Mary, conceived without sin, pray for us who have recourse to you.
O Mary, by your pure and Immaculate Conception, make my body pure and my soul holy.
Jesus, Mary and Joseph, I give you my heart and my soul.
Jesus, Mary and Joseph, assist me in my last agony.
Jesus, Mary and Joseph, May I die in peace, and in your blessed company.

Holy Mary, pray for us sinners, now and at the hour of our death.
Mother of God, pray for us.
Holy Mary, pray for us.
Queen of the most holy Rosary, pray for us.
Mary, refuge of sinners, bring all sinners back to Christ.
Our Lady of Sorrow, help me to overcome my problem.
Blessed be the name of Mary.
Our Lady of Guadalupe, help us to abolish abortion.
Holy Mary, our hope, seat of wisdom, pray for us.
Heart of Jesus, formed by the Holy Spirit in the womb of the Virgin Mother, pray for us.
Queen of Angels, our help in all our necessities, pray for us.

10

Mary Leads Us to the Eucharist

On August 15, 1996, the Holy Father gave the following message to those who were attending his audience at Castelgandolfo. It was a message he had sent to Czestochowa in his native Poland, to the 19th International Marian Congress to take place on August 24-26.

Hail, Jesus, Son of Mary, in the sacred Host you are the true God.

Joining in spirit with those attending the 19th International Marian Congress, I recall the words from a hymn that in Poland often accompanies eucharistic adoration and processions. I repeat them because they contain the truth that, together with praising Christ present in the mystery of the Eucharist, almost of necessity we recall the memory of the Mother of God.

It is thanks to her generous *fiat* that the Word of God was made flesh by the work of the Holy Spirit. She offered her own body to the Word so that he might take it upon himself and the miracle of the divine Incarnation would be accomplished. In her virginal womb Mary bore the Incarnate Word, awaiting *with love beyond all telling* the birth of the Savior - as the liturgy states (Preface of Advent II).

When she gave birth to the Son of God, she was, in a certain sense, the first to worship his presence among men. Together with Joseph she took the divine Child to the Temple to offer him to God, according to the prescriptions of the law. Even then, through the words of Simeon, God had revealed to her that the sword of sorrow would pierce her heart, when her Son became the sign of contradiction *for the fall and rising of many* (Lk 2 34).

This was the announcement of Mary's participation in the saving work of Christ, Priest and Victim, which was to be accomplished on Golgotha. *At the foot of the cross, out of love for your Son, she extended her motherhood to all men, born again by the death of Christ for a life that will never end. . . . Taken up into heavenly glory, with maternal love she accompanies the Church and protects her on the way to her homeland until the glorious day of the Lord* (Italian Missal, Preface of the Blessed Virgin Mary III).

Mary's Participation

Every Holy Mass makes present in an unbloody manner that unique and perfect sacrifice, offered by Christ on the tree of the cross, in which Mary participated, joined in spirit with her suffering Son, lovingly consenting to his sacrifice and offering her own sorrow to the Father (cf. *Lumen Gentium*, n. 58).

Therefore, when we celebrate the Eucharist, the memorial of Christ's passover, the memory of his Mother's suffering is also made alive and present, this Mother who, as an unsurpassable model, teaches the faithful to unite themselves more intimately to the sacrifice of her Son, the one Redeemer.

Through spiritual communion with the sorrowful Mother of God, believers share in a special way in the paschal mystery and are opened to this extraordinary action of the Holy Spirit which produces a supernatural joy because of communion with the glorious Christ, on the example of the joy granted to Mary in the glory of heaven, as the first person to share in the fruits of the redemption.

Mary and the Eucharist

The organizers of the 19th International Marian Congress in Jasna Gora proposed this as a theme for study and prayer. And it is a correct choice, especially in view of the international eucharistic congress that will be held next year in Krakow.

In this way, just as Mary is present at the beginning of the mission of the Incarnate Word, and thereby at the origins of the Eucharist as well, the Marian congress this year marks the start of the Church's spiritual preparation to make the eucharistic congress a fruitful experience.

May these days bring you all close to she who - throughout her life in communion with her Son, not only by ties of blood but especially by love - is the perfect teacher of that love which enables us to be united in the deepest way with Christ in the mystery of his Eucharistic Presence. Let Mary lead us to the Eucharist!

Mary's Protection

I ask all of you who are gathered in Jasna Gora for the Marian congress to pray for the intentions of the Church and the world. As we give thanks for 20 centuries of Mary's protection of the Church, let us together ask her to lead believers toward an ever more perfect knowledge of the saving power of the sacrifice of Christ, who is present in the Eucharist. Let us pray that the living experience of communion with Christ may bear fruits of zeal in the hearts of all Christians as they build up a communion of love among men.

May the Mother of God lead us into the third millennium, united around the Word of God who was made flesh in her.

I cordially bless you all.

11

Our Lady and Vatican II

When Pope John XXIII announced his intention of invoking the Second Vatican Ecumenical Council on January 25, 1959, he asked that above all we must *trust in the intercession of the Immaculate Mother of Jesus and our Mother for its success*; and when he set the opening date as October 11, 1962, he did so to tie it to the memory of the Council of Ephesus in 431, whose decisions upheld belief in the Virgin Mary as Mother of God. October 11 is the feast of the Divine Maternity of Mary. The Council was formally invoked on February 2, 1962, the feast of the Purification of the Blessed Virgin.

On the day the Council opened, Pope John XXIII reminded the Council Fathers that the Council was being opened under the auspices of the Virgin Mother of God. The first session closed on December

8, the feast of the Immaculate Conception when the Pope pointed out that *many of the Church's great events take place in Mary's presence, in testimony and assurance of her motherly protection.*

Pope John XXIII died on June 3, 1963. On September 12, the feast of the most Holy Name of Mary, our new Holy Father, Pope Paul VI stated that the Council's second session would start on the feast of St Michael the Archangel, September 29, where he said: *Here certainly the Virgin Mother of Christ is helping us from heaven.*

It was in the second session also that the Council Fathers voted that greater emphasis should be put on the preeminent role of the Blessed Virgin in the Church's liturgical cycle (see Chapter V, *Constitution on the Sacred Liturgy).*

During the third session the debate on the eight chapter of *The Constitution on the Church,* the most important of the 16 documents of the Council, lasted two days. The document states: *It does not intend to give a complete doctrine on Mary, nor does it wish to decide those questions which the work of theologians has not yet clarified* (#54). It was at this session that the Holy Father proclaimed Mary as Mother of the Church.

Throughout the Council the presence of Our Lady was very much evident, sessions beginning and ending on her feast days, while she was continually invoked. On December 8, 1965, again on the feast of the Immaculate Conception, the Council was officially closed with a Mass celebrated by Pope Paul VI, at the end of which he blessed the foundation stone which would be used in the church to commemorate the Council and dedicated to the Blessed Virgin.

The eighth chapter of *Lumen Gentium, The Constitution on the Church,* is devoted to Our Lady and called *The Blessed Virgin Mary, Mother of God, in the Mystery of Christ and the Church.* It is what the Second Vatican Council said concerning Our Lady. The subheads have been added to the official Latin text.

(I) INTRODUCTION
The Blessed Virgin in the Mystery of Christ

52. Wishing in his supreme goodness and wisdom to effect the redemption of the world, *when the fullness of time came, God sent his Son, born of a woman ... that we might receive the adoption of sons* (Gal 4 4). *He for us men, and for our salvation, came down from heaven, and was incarnated by the Holy*

Spirit from the Virgin Mary.[1] This divine mystery of salvation is revealed to us and continued in the Church, which the Lord established as his body. Joined to Christ the head and in communion with all his saints, the faithful must in the first place reverence the memory *of the glorious ever Virgin Mary, Mother of God and of our Lord Jesus Christ.*[2]

53. The Virgin Mary, who at the message of the angel received the Word of God in her heart and in her body and gave Life to the world, is acknowledged and honored as being truly the Mother of God and of the redeemer. Redeemed, in a more exalted fashion, by reason of the merits of her Son and united to him by a close and indissoluble tie, she is endowed with the high office and dignity of the Mother of the Son of God, and therefore she is also the beloved daughter of the Father and temple of the Holy Spirit. Because of this gift of sublime grace she far surpasses all creatures, both in heaven and on earth. But, being of the race of Adam, she is at the same time also united to all those who are to be saved; indeed, *she is clearly the mother of the members of Christ . . . since she has by her charity joined in bringing about the birth of believers in the Church, who are members of its head.*[3] Wherefore she is hailed as pre-eminent

and as a wholly unique member of the Church, and as its type and outstanding model in faith and charity. The Catholic Church taught by the Holy Spirit, honors her with filial affection and devotion as a most beloved mother

Intention of the Council

54. Wherefore this sacred synod, while expounding the doctrine on the Church, in which the divine redeemer brings about our salvation, intends to set forth painstakingly both the role of the Blessed Virgin in the mystery of the Incarnate Word and the Mystical Body, and the duties of the redeemed towards the Mother of God, who is mother of Christ and mother of men, and most of all of those who believe. It does not, however, intend to give a complete doctrine on Mary, nor does it wish to decide those questions which the work of theologians has not yet fully clarified. Those opinions therefore may be lawfully retained which are propounded in Catholic schools concerning her, who occupies a place in the Church which is the highest after Christ and also the closest to us.[4]

(II) THE FUNCTION OF THE BLESSED VIRGIN IN THE PLAN OF SALVATION

Mother of the Messiah in the Old Testament

55. The sacred writings of the Old and New Testaments, as well as venerable tradition, show the role of the Mother of the Savior in the plan of salvation in an ever clearer light and call our attention to it. The books of the Old Testament describe the history of salvation, by which the coming of Christ into the world was slowly prepared. The earliest documents, as they are read in the Church and are understood in the light of a further and full revelation, bring the figure of the woman, Mother of the Redeemer, into a gradually clearer light. Considered in this light, she is already prophetically foreshadowed in the promise of victory over the serpent which was given to our first parents after their fall into sin (cf. Gen 3 15). Likewise she is the virgin who shall conceive and bear a son, whose name shall be called Emmanuel (c. Is 8 14; Mic 5 2-3; Mt 1 22-23). She stands out among the poor and humble of the Lord, who confidently hope for and receive salvation from him. After a long period of waiting the times are fulfilled in her, the exalted Daughter of Sion and the new plan of salvation is established, when the Son of God took

human nature from her, that he might in the mysteries of his flesh free man from sin.

Mary in the Annunciation

56. The Father of mercies willed that the Incarnation should be preceded by assent on the part of the predestined mother, so that just as a woman had a share in bringing about death, so also a woman should contribute to life. This is preeminently true of the Mother of Jesus, who gave to the world the Life that renews all things, and who was enriched by God with gifts appropriate to such a role. It is no wonder then that it was customary for the Fathers to refer to the Mother of God as all holy and free from every stain of sin, as though fashioned by the Holy Spirit and formed as a new creature.[5] Enriched from the first instant of her conception with the splendor of an entirely unique holiness, the virgin of Nazareth is hailed by the heralding angel, by divine command, as *full of grace* (cf. Lk 1 28), and to the heavenly messenger she replies: *Behold the handmaid of the Lord, be it done unto me according to thy word* (Lk 1 38). Thus the daughter of Adam, Mary, consenting to the word of God, became the Mother of Jesus. Committing herself wholeheartedly and impeded by

no sin to God's saving will, she devoted herself totally, as a handmaid of the Lord, to the person and work of her Son, under him and with him, serving the mystery of redemption, by the grace of Almighty God. Rightly, therefore, the Fathers see Mary not merely as passively engaged by God, but as freely co-operating in the work of man's salvation through faith and obedience. For, as St Irenaeus says, she *being obedient, became the cause of salvation for herself and for the whole human race.*[6] Hence not a few of the early Fathers assert with him in their preaching: *the knot of Eve's disobedience was untied by Mary's obedience; what the virgin Eve bound through her unbelief, Mary loosened by her faith.*[7] Comparing Mary with Eve, they call her *Mother of the living,*[8] and frequently claim: *death through Eve, life through Mary.*[9]

The Blessed Virgin and the Infant Jesus

57.   This union of the mother with the Son in the work of salvation is made manifest from the time of Christ's virginal conception up to his death; first when Mary, arising in haste to go to visit Elizabeth, is greeted by her as blessed because of her belief in the promise of salvation and the precursor leaped with joy

in the womb of his mother (cf. Lk 1 41-45); then also at the birth of Our Lord, who did not diminish his mother's virginal integrity but sanctified it,[10] the Mother of God joyfully showed her first-born son to the shepherds and the Magi; when she presented him to the Lord in the temple, making the offering of the poor, she heard Simeon foretelling at the same time that her Son would be a sign of contradiction and that a sword would pierce the mother's soul, that out of many hearts thoughts might be revealed (cf. Lk 2 34-35); when the child Jesus was lost and they had sought him sorrowing, his parents found him in the temple, engaged in the things that were his Father's, and they did not understand the words of their Son. His mother, however, kept all these things to be pondered in her heart (cf. Lk 2 41-51).

The Blessed Virgin and the Public Ministry of Jesus

58. In the public life of Jesus, Mary appears prominently; at the very beginning when at the marriage feast of Cana, moved with pity, she brought about by her intercession the beginning of miracles of Jesus the Messiah (cf. Jn 2 1-11). In the course of her Son's preaching she received the words whereby, in

extolling a kingdom beyond the concerns and ties of flesh and blood, he declared blessed those who heard and kept the word of God (cf. Mk 3 35; par. Lk 11 27-28) as she was faithfully doing (cf. Lk 2 19; 51). Thus the Blessed Virgin advanced in her pilgrimage of faith, and faithfully persevered in union with her Son unto the cross, where she stood, in keeping with the divine plan, enduring with her only begotten Son the intensity of his suffering, associated herself with his sacrifice in her mother's heart and lovingly consenting to the immolation of this victim which was born of her. Finally, she was given by the same Christ Jesus dying on the cross as a mother to his disciple, with these words: *Woman, behold thy son* (Jn 19 26-27).[11]

The Blessed Virgin after the Ascension

59. But since it had pleased God not to manifest solemnly the mystery of the salvation of the human race before he would pour forth the Spirit promised by Christ, we see the apostles before the day of Pentecost *persevering with one mind in prayer with the women and Mary the Mother of Jesus, and with his brethren* (Acts 1 14), and we also see Mary by her prayers imploring the gift of the Spirit, who had already overshadowed her in the Annunciation.

Finally the Immaculate Virgin preserved free from all stain of original sin,[12] was taken up body and soul into heavenly glory,[13] when her earthly life was over, and exalted by the Lord as Queen over all things, that she might be the more fully conformed to her Son, the Lord of lords (cf. Rev 19 16) and conqueror of sin and death.[14]

(III) THE BLESSED VIRGIN AND THE CHURCH

Mary Handmaid of the Lord and Savior

60.　　In the words of the apostle there is but one mediator: *for there is but one God and one mediator of God and men, the man Christ Jesus, who gave himself a redemption for all* (I Tim 2 5-6). But Mary's function as mother of men in no way obscures or diminishes this unique mediation of Christ, but rather shows its power. But the Blessed Virgin's salutary influence on men originates not in any inner necessity but in the disposition of God. It flows forth from the superabundance of the merits of Christ, rests on his mediation, depends entirely on it and draws all its power from it. It does not hinder in any way the immediate union of the faithful with Christ but on the contrary fosters it.

61. The predestination of the Blessed Virgin as Mother of God was associated with the Incarnation of the Divine Word: in the designs of divine providence she was the gracious mother of the divine redeemer here on earth, and above all others and in a singular way the generous associate and humble handmaid of the Lord. She conceived, brought forth, and nourished Christ, she presented him to the Father in the temple, shared her Son's sufferings as he died on the cross. Thus, in a wholly singular way she co-operated by her obedience, faith, hope and burning charity in the work of the Savior in restoring supernatural life to souls. For this reason she is a mother to us in the order of grace.

62. This motherhood of Mary in the order of grace continued uninterruptedly from the consent which she loyally gave at the Annunciation and which she sustained without wavering beneath the cross, until the eternal fulfilment of all the elect. Taken up to heaven she did not lay aside this saving office but by her manifold intercession continues to bring us the gifts of eternal salvation.[15] By her maternal charity, she cares for the brethren of her Son, who still journey on earth surrounded by dangers and difficulties, until they are led into their blessed home. Therefore the

Blessed Virgin is invoked in the Church under the titles of advocate, helper, benefactress, and mediatrix.[16] This, however is so understood that it neither takes away anything from nor adds anything to the dignity and efficacy of Christ the one mediator.[17]

No creature could ever be counted along with the Incarnate Word and Redeemer; but just as the priesthood of Christ is shared in various ways both by his ministers and the faithful, and as the one goodness of God is radiated in different ways among his creatures, so also the unique mediation of the redeemer does not exclude but rather gives rise to a manifold co-operation which is but a sharing in this one source.

The Church does not hesitate to profess this subordinate role of Mary, which it constantly experiences and recommends to the heartfelt attention of the faithful, so that encouraged by this maternal help they may the more closely adhere to the mediator and redeemer.

Mary, Type of the Church as Virgin and Mother
63. By reason of the gift and role of her divine motherhood by which she is united with her Son, the redeemer, and with her unique graces and

functions, the Blessed Virgin is also intimately united to the Church. As St Ambrose taught, the Mother of God is a type of the Church in the order of faith, charity, and perfect union with Christ.[18] For in the mystery of the Church, which is itself rightly called mother and virgin, the Blessed Virgin stands out in eminent and singular fashion as exemplar both of virgin and mother.[19] Through her faith and obedience she gave birth on earth to the very Son of the Father, not through the knowledge of man but by the overshadowing of the Holy Spirit, in the manner of a new Eve who placed her faith, not in the serpent of old but in God's messenger without wavering in doubt. The Son whom she brought forth is he whom God place as the first-born among many brethren (Rom 8 29), that is, the faithful in whose generation and formation she co-operates with a mother's love.

64. The Church indeed contemplating her hidden sanctity, imitating her charity and faithfully fulfilling the Father's will, by receiving the word of God in faith becomes herself a mother. By preaching and baptism she brings forth sons, who are conceived of the Holy Spirit and born of God, to a new and immortal life. She herself is a virgin, who keeps in its entirety and purity the faith she pledged to her spouse.

Imitating the mother of her Lord, and by the power of the Holy Spirit, she keeps intact faith, firm hope and sincere charity.[20]

Mary's Virtues, Model for the Church

65. But while in the most Blessed Virgin the Church has already reached that perfection whereby she exists without spot or wrinkle (cf. Eph 5 27), the faithful still strive to conquer sin and increase in holiness. And so they turn their eyes to Mary who shines forth to the whole community of the elect as the model of virtues. Devoutly meditating on her and contemplating her in the light of the Word made man, the Church reverently penetrates more deeply into the great mystery of the Incarnation and becomes more and more like her spouse. Having entered deeply into the history of salvation, Mary, in a way, unites in her person and re-echoes the most important doctrines of the faith: and when she is the subject of preaching and worship she prompts the faithful to come to her Son, to his sacrifice and to the love of the Father. Seeking after the glory of Christ, the Church becomes more like her lofty type, and continually progresses in faith, hope and charity, seeking and doing the will of God in all things. The Church, therefore, in her apostolic

work too, rightly looks to her who gave birth to Christ, who was thus conceived of the Holy Spirit and born of a virgin, in order that through the Church he could be born and increase in the hearts of the faithful. In her life the Virgin has been a model of that motherly love with which love all who join in the Church's apostolic mission for the regeneration of mankind should be animated.

(IV) THE CULT OF THE BLESSED VIRGIN IN THE CHURCH

Nature and Basis of the Devotion to the Blessed Virgin

66. Mary has by grace been exalted above all angels and men to a place second only to her Son, as the most holy Mother of God who was involved in the mysteries of Christ: she is rightly honored by a special cult in the Church. From the earliest times the Blessed Virgin is honored under the title of Mother of God, whose protection the faithful take refuge together in prayer in all their perils and needs.[21] Accordingly, following the Council of Ephesus, there was a remarkable growth in the cult of the People of God towards Mary, in veneration and love, in invocation and imitation, according to her own

prophetic words: *all generations shall call me blessed, because he that is mighty hath done great things to me* (Lk 1 48). This cult, as it has always existed in the Church, for all its uniqueness, differs essentially from the cult of adoration, which is offered equally to the Incarnate Word and to the Father and the Holy Spirit, and it is most favorable to it. The various forms of piety towards the Mother of God, which the Church has approved within the limits of sound and orthodox doctrine, ensure that while the mother is honored, the Son through whom all things have their being (cf. Col 1 15-16) and in whom it has pleased the Father that all fullness should dwell (cf. Col 1 19), is rightly known, loved and glorified and his commandments are observed.

Devotion to Mary Encouraged

67. The sacred synod teaches this Catholic doctrine advisedly and at the same time admonishes all the sons of the Church that the cult, especially the liturgical cult, of the Blessed Virgin, be generously fostered, and that the practices and exercises of devotion towards her, recommended by the magisterium of the Church in the course of centuries be highly esteemed, and that those decrees, which

have been given in the early days regarding the cult of images of Christ, the Blessed Virgin and the saints, be religiously observed.[22] But it strongly urges theologians and preachers of the word of God to be careful to refrain as much from all false exaggeration as from too summary an attitude in considering the special dignity of the Mother of God.[23] Following the study of Sacred Scripture, the Fathers, the doctors and liturgy of the Church, and under the guidance of the Church's magisterium, let them rightly illustrate the duties and privileges of the Blessed Virgin which always refer to Christ, the source of all truth, sanctity, and devotion. Let them carefully refrain from whatever might by word or deed lead the separated brethren or any others whatsoever into error about the true doctrine of the Church. Let the faithful remember moreover that true devotion consists neither in sterile or transitory affection, nor in a certain vain credulity, but proceeds from true faith, by which we are led to recognize the excellence of the Mother of God, and we are moved to a filial love towards our mother and to the imitation of her virtues.

(V) MARY, SIGN OF TRUE HOPE AND COMFORT FOR THE PILGRIM PEOPLE OF GOD

68. In the meantime the Mother of Jesus in the glory which she possesses in body and soul in heaven is the image and beginning of the Church as it is to be perfected in the world to come. Likewise she shines forth on earth, until the day of the Lord shall come (cf. Pet 3 10), a sign of certain hope and comfort to the pilgrim People of God.

69. It gives great joy and comfort to this sacred synod that among the separated brethren too there are those who give due honor to the Mother of Our Lord and Savior, especially among the Easterns, who with devout mind and fervent impulse give honor to the Mother of God, ever virgin.[24] The entire body of the faithful pours forth urgent supplications to the Mother of God and men that she, who aided the beginnings of the Church by her prayers, may now, exalted as she is above all the angels and saints, intercede before her Son in the fellowship of all the saints, until all families of people, whether they are honored with the title of Christian or whether they still do not know the savior, may be happily gathered together in peace and harmony into one People of

God, for the glory of the Most Holy and undivided Trinity.

Each and every utterance in this dogmatic constitution has been endorsed by the Fathers. And we, in virtue of the apostolic power entrusted to us by Christ, in union with the venerable Fathers, in the Holy Spirit, approve, decree, and enact them; and we order that the enactments of this synod be promulgated for the glory of God.

NOTES

[1] Creed of the Roman Mass; Symbol of Constantinople; Mansi 3, 566, Cf. Council of Ephesus, **ibid.** 4, 1130 (**et ibid.** 2, 665 and 4, 1071); Council of Chalcedon, **ibid.** 7, 111-116; Council of Constantinople II, **ibid,** 9, 375-396.

[2] Canon of the Roman Mass.

[3] Cf. Saint Augustine, **De S. Virginitate**, 6: P.L., 40, 399.

[4] Cf. Pope Paul VI, **Allocution to the Council**, 4 December 1963: A.A.S. 56 (1964), p. 37.

[5] Cf. Saint Germanus of Constantinople, **Hom, in Annunt, Deiparae**: P.G. 98, 328 A; **In Dorm.** 2 Col. 357. Anastasius of Antioch, Serm. 2 **de Annunt**. 2: P.G. 89, 1377 AB; **Serm.** 3. 2: Col. 1388 C. Saint Andrew of Crete, **Can in B.V. Nat.** 4: P.G. 97, 1321 B. **In B.V. Nat.** 1: Col. 812 A. **Hom. In Dorm.** 1: Col. 1068 C. Saint Sophronius, Or. 2 **in Annunt.** 18: P.G. 87 (3), 3237 BD.

[6] Saint Ireneaus, **Adv. Haer.** III, 22, 4: P.G. 7, 959 A, Harvey, 2, 123.

[7] Saint Irenaeus, **ibid.**: Harvey, 2, 124.

[8] Saint Epiphanius, **Haer.** 78, 18: P.G. 42, 728 CD-729 AB.

[9] Saint Jerome, **Epist.** 22, 21: P.L. 22, 408, Cf. Saint Augustine, **Serm.** 51, 2, 3: P.L. 38, 335; **Serm.** 232, 2: Col. 1108. Saint Cyril of Jerusalem, **Catech.** 12, 15: P.G. 33, 741 AB, Saint John Chrysostom, **In Ps. 44**, 7: P.G. 55, 193. Saint John Damascene, Hom 2 **in Dorm. B.M.V.**, 3: P.G. 96,728.

[10] Cf. Council of Lateran A.D. 649, Can. 3: Mansi 10, 1151. Saint Leo the Great, **Epist. Ad. Flav.**: P.L. 54, 759. Council of Chalcedon: Mansi 7, 462. Saint Ambrose, **De instit. Virg.**: P.L. 16, 320.

[11] Cf. Pius XII, Encycl. **Mystici Corpori,** 29 June 1943: A.A.S. 35 (1943), pp. 247-248.

[12] Cf. Pius IX, Bull **Ineffabilis**, 8 Dec. 1854: **Acta Pii IX**, 1, 1, p. 616; Denz 1641 (2803).

[13] Cf. Pius XII, Const. Apost. **Munificentissimus**, 1 Nov. 1950: A.A.S.

42 (1950): Denz. 2333 (3903). Cf. Saint John Damascene, **Enc. In dorm. Dei Genitrichs, Hom.** 2 and 3: P.G. 96, 722-762, especially Col. 728 B. Saint Germanus of Constantinople, **In S. Dei gen. dorm. Serm. 1**: P.G. 98 (6), 340-348; **Serm. 3**: Col. 362. Saint Modestus of Jerusalem, **In dorm. SS. Deiparae**: P.G. 86 (2), 3277-3312.

[14] Cf. Pius XII, Encycl. **Ad coeli Reginam,** 11 Oct. 1954: A.A.S. 46 (1954), pp. 633-636; Denz. 3913 ff. Cf. Saint Andrew of Crete, **Hom. 3 in dorm. SS. Deiparae**: P.G. 97, 1990-1109. Saint John Damascene, **De fide orth.,** IV, 14: P.G. 94, 1153-1168.

[15] Cf.Kleutgen, corrected text **De mysterio verbi incarnati,** chap. IV: Mans 53, 290. Cf. Saint Andrew of Crete, **In nat. Mariae, Serm. 4**: P.G. 97, 865 A. Saint Germanus of Constantinople, **In ann. Deiparae**: P.G. 93, 322 BC. **In dorm. Deiparae** III: Col. 362 D. Saint John Damascene, **In dorm. B.V. Mariae, Hom.** 1, 8: P.G. 96, 712 BC-713 A.

[16] Cf. Leo XIII, Encycl. **Adjutricem populi,** 5 Sept. 1895: A.A.S. 15 (1895-1896), p. 303. Saint Pius X, Encycl. **Ad diem illum.** 2 Feb. 1904: **Acta** 1, p. 154; Denz. 1978 a (3370). Pius XI, Encycl. **Miserentissimus,** 8 May 1928; A.A.S., 20 (1928), p. 178. Pius XII, Radio Message, 13 May 1946: A.A.S. 38 (1946), p. 266.

[17] Saint Ambrose, **Epist.** 63: P.L. 16, 1218.

[18] Saint Ambrose, **Expos. Le. II,** 7: P.O. 15, 1555.

[19] Cf. Pseudo Peter Damien, **Serm.** 63: P.L. 1444, 861 AB. Geoffrey (De Breteuil) of Saint Victor, **In nat. b.m.,** MS. Paris, Mazarine, 1002, fol 109 r. Gerhoch of Reichersberg, **De gloria et honore Filii hominis** 10: P.L. 194, 1105 AB.

[20] Saint Ambrose, l.c., and **Expos. Le. X,** 24-25: P.L. 15, 1810. Saint Augustine, **In Jo. Tr** 13, 12: P.L. 35, 1499. Cf. **Serm.** 191, 2, 3: P.L. 38, 1010, etc. Cf. Also Ven. Bede, **In Le. Expo.,** 1, chap. II: 92, 330 Isaac of Stella, **Serm.** 31: P.L. 194, 1863 A.

[21] '**Sub tuum praesidium.**'

[22] Council of Nicea II. A.D. 787: Mansi 13, 378-379; Denz. 302 (600-601). Council of Trent, Sess. 25: Mansi 33, 171-172.

[23] Cf. Pius XII, Radio Message, 24 Oct. 1954: A.A.S. 46 (1954), p. 679 Encycl. **Ad coeli Reginam,** 11 Oct. 1954: A.A.S. 46 (1954), p. 637.

[24] Cf. Pius XI, Encycl. **Ecclesiam Dei,** 12 Nov. 1923: A.A.S. 15 (1923), p. 581; Pius XII, Encycl. **Fulgens corona,** 8 Sept. 1953: A.A.S. 45 (1953), p. 590-591.

BIBLIOGRAPHY

Ball, Ann, *Blessed Miguel Pro: 20th-Century Mexican Martyr*, Tan Books and Publishers, Inc., Rockford, IL, 1996.

Belmonte, Rev. Charles and Socia, Rev. James, *Handbook of Prayers*, Scepter Publishers, Princeton, NJ, 1992.

Benedictine Monks of Solesmes, *Our Lady*, St Paul Editions, Boston, MA, 1961.

Catechism of the Catholic Church, Ignatius Press, San Francisco, CA, 1994.

Del Mazza, S.D.B., Rev. Valentino, *Our Lady Among Us*, St Paul Editions, Boston, MA, 1961.

De Montfort, St Louis, *The Secret of the Rosary*, Montfort Publications, Bay Shore, NY, 1965.

Duffner, M.S.C., Rev., *Sorrowful and Immaculate Heart of Mary*, World Apostolate of Fatima, Washington, NJ.

Escriva, Blessed Josemaria, *Holy Rosary*, Scepter, Chicago, IL, 1953.

Flannery, O.P., Rev. Austin, *Vatican Council II, Vol. 1*, The Liturgical Press, Collegeville, MN, 1982.

Garrigou Lagrance, O.P., Rev. Reginald, *The Mother of Our Savior*, Tan Books and Publishers, Inc., Rockford, IL, 1993.

Legion of Mary, *The Official Handbook*, Dublin, 1953.

Miravalle, Mark I, S.T.D., *Mary:CoRedemptrix, Mediatrix, Advocate*, Queenship Publishing, Santa Barbara, CA, 1993.

Sharkey, Don, *The Woman Shall Conquer*, Prow Books, Kenosha, WI, 1973.

Socias, Rev. James, *Daily Roman Missal*, Scepter Publishers, Princeton, NJ, 1993.

Suarez, Rev. Federico, *Mary of Nazareth*, Scepter, Chicago, IL, 1960.

Walsh, William Thomas, *Our Lady of Fatima*, Doubleday, New York, NY, 1947.

Other Devotional Books

DEVOTION TO THE SACRED HEART OF JESUS
by. W. Doyle Gilligan
A very up to the minute book on the devotion to the Sacred Heart of Jesus and how it is most important for our day. It includes both prayers and the history of the devotion.

Paper $5.95

DEVOTION TO THE HOLY ANGELS
ed. W. Doyle Gilligan
With a growing interest in angels this book is most timely. It contains a wonderful collection of prayers, novenas, and litanies to the angels. It is now in its second printing.

Paper $4.95

DEVOTION TO THE HOLY SOULS IN PURGATORY
by W. Doyle Gilligan
This book has been put together to foster a greater understanding about Purgatory and also to help spread devotion to the holy souls there. It explains the great spiritual benefits that can be received by those who have devotion to the holy souls and contains both devotional practices and doctrinal information.

Paper $4.95

Please add $1.50 for shipping for the first book and 50¢ for each thereafter. Thank you.

Order from **Lumen Christi Press**,
P. O. Box 130176, Houston, TX 77219
or from your local bookstore.